Grade 6
Poetry
Comprehension Skills

MW01156687

Contents

Poetry Comprehension Skills

Introduction

This book is designed to help students become better readers through the reading of poetry. The IRA/NCTE Standards for the English Language Arts list as the first recommendation: "Students read a wide range of print and nonprint texts to build an understanding of texts, of themselves, and of the cultures of the United States and the world…." Poetry is a form of literature easily read and enjoyed by students of all ages. Children's books often use the rhythm and rhyme of poetry to engage young readers. Poetry helps develop language skills and is often used in phonemic awareness techniques. Moreover, since poetry often uses figurative speech, it encourages imagination and creative thinking. As students progress, their enjoyment of poetry grows to encompass different forms and styles. Most students not only enjoy reading poetry, but they enjoy creating their own verse as well. Finally, most assessment tests now include poetry. These tests include both multiple choice and short-answer questions. It is important that students become comfortable with the format so they are confident when they encounter it in testing situations.

The Poetry Series

This reproducible poetry series will supplement any reading program. Each lesson tests comprehension skills as well as offers suggestions for vocabulary and fluency development, two essential skills for reading and language development.

Organization of the Poetry Series

The book is divided into four thematic units which will help the teacher integrate poetry into other content areas. The units are On the Silly Side; People, Young and Old; Nature-ally Fun; and Tales to Tell. There are five poems in each unit. The lesson components are explained below.

Teacher Information

The first page of every lesson provides explicit instructions for teaching the poem. There are specific sections that address multiple skills. To begin, each poem is summarized. A list of words that children may find difficult to read or understand is included as well. Another section lists a specific poetry standard and outlines an activity that will help students explore the concept. A third section outlines how to introduce the poem and the vocabulary words, and it also includes ideas for fluency practice. Finally, a fun and creative writing suggestion helps children think about the topic or a specific skill to extend the lesson.

Poem

The poems were selected to complement topics taught at each grade level. Illustrations on the page support the topic to help children better understand the content.

Assessment

Each poem is followed by a seven-question assessment. The first six questions are in a standardized-test format and focus on six important comprehension skills. They always follow a prescribed order:

1. Facts The first question focuses on literal comprehension. Students identify pieces of factual information. They look for details that tell who, what, when, where, and how.

2. Sequence The second question refers to sequence. Students practice identifying the order of events or the steps in a process.

3. Context In the third question, students are required to practice using all the words in the poem to understand unfamiliar words. Students become aware of the relationships between words, phrases, and sentences.

4. Main Idea In this question, students will identify the overall point made in the poem. Students must be able to differentiate between the main idea and details.

5. Conclusion The fifth question requires students to draw conclusions. Conclusions are not stated in the reading but must be formulated. Students draw conclusions based only on the information in the poem.

6. Inference The sixth question asks students to make inferences by combining their own knowledge and experience with what they read. They put the facts together to make a reasonable inference about something that is not stated in the poem.

7. Short Answer The final question requires that children write a brief response to a higher-level question.

Other Components

• **Standards** A list of grade-level, poetry-specific standards is found on page 5. A chart highlights in which lesson each standard is introduced.

• **Glossary** Poetry terms and definitions for use by the teacher and older students are given on page 6. Some of the elements are not introduced to younger students in this poetry series since they require advanced knowledge.

• **General Assessment** A two-page assessment is found on pages 7 and 8. It can be used as a pretest to gauge students' understanding of the comprehension skills. It can also be used as a posttest to determine improvements after exposure to poetic literature.

• **Graphic Organizers** Five graphic organizers are provided on pages 9–13 to support different activities and skill development suggested in various lessons.

Poetry Standards • Grade 6

The following standards focus specifically on poetry and are accepted by many states as important to students in the sixth grade.

Standard	Lesson
Identify and analyze the characteristics of fiction, nonfiction, poetry, and plays	1
Identify rhyme	8, 15
Identify rhythm	5, 19
Recognize the use of repetition in poetry	4
Identify a haiku poem	14
Identify a free verse poem	18
Identify a narrative poem	3, 16
Identify a diamante	9
Identify a ballad	17
Recognize the use of figurative language (simile, metaphor, personification, dialect)	2, 6, 7, 10, 11, 13, 20
Identify words that develop auditory skills (alliteration, onomatopoeia, assonance, consonance)	12
Describe elements of story structure in fiction and poetry (characterization, setting, events of the plot, and solution)	All poems
Read stories, poems, and passages with fluency utilizing appropriate rhythm, pacing, intonation, and expression	All poems

Standards
Poetry: Grade 6, SV 9896-5

Glossary

alliteration the repetition of the same beginning sound, usually a consonant, in a phrase or line of poetry. Tongue twisters use alliteration. Example: *She sells seashells by the seashore.*

analogy a likeness between two things that are not alike in other ways. Example: *the wings of a bird and the arms of a person*

assonance the repetition of similar vowel sounds in words so they are close in sound but do not rhyme. Example: *She feeds the deer.*

ballad a long poem written about a famous person or event

cinquain a formula poem that has five lines and a total of 22 syllables, distributed in a specific 2–4–6–8–2 pattern

concrete a poem in which the words, letters, or shape of the poem matches the topic

consonance the close repetition of identical consonant sounds before and after different vowels. Example: *flip—flop; feel—fill*

diamante a formula poem that is shaped like a diamond, and the words describe opposite ideas

haiku a formula poem that has three lines and a total of 17 syllables, often distributed in a specific 5–7–5 pattern

imagery the author's use of description and words to create pictures in the reader's mind

limerick a humorous formula poem that has five lines, an "aabba" rhyming pattern, and a specific rhythm

metaphor the comparison of two things in which one is said to be another. Metaphors do not use the words *like* or *as*. Example: *The lake was a golden mirror.*

meter the cadence, or beat, of a poem, determined by regular patterns of heavily and lightly stressed syllables

onomatopoeia a sound device in which a word makes the sound. Examples: *crash, bang*

personification a device in which human qualities and ideas are given to things. Example: *The wind whispered through the trees.*

poetry an expression of ideas or feeling in words. Poetry usually has form, rhythm, and rhyme.

repetition a sound device in which sounds, words, or phrases are repeated to emphasize a point

rhyme two or more lines that end with rhyming words

rhyming words words that end in the same sounds

rhythm the repeated meter, or beat, in a poem

simile the comparison of two things that are not really alike by using the words *like* or *as*. Example: *Her smile was like sunshine.*

sonnet a poem with 14 lines and a specific rhyming and rhythm pattern

stanza a group of related lines in a poem

tanka a formula poem that has five lines and a total of 31 syllables, distributed in a specific 5–7–5–7–7 pattern

tone choice of words and phrasing to show the author's attitude or feeling

The Rainy Day

by Henry Wadsworth Longfellow

The day is cold, and dark, and dreary;
It rains, and the wind is never weary;
The vine still clings to the mouldering wall,
But at every gust the dead leaves fall,
    And the day is dark and dreary.

My life is cold, and dark, and dreary;
It rains, and the wind is never weary;
My thoughts still cling to the mouldering Past,
But the hopes of youth fall thick in the blast,
    And the days are dark and dreary.

Be still, sad heart! and cease repining;
Behind the clouds is the sun still shining;
Thy fate is the common fate of all,
Into each life some rain must fall,
    Some days must be dark and dreary.

Go on to the next page.

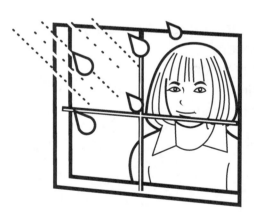

The Rainy Day: Assessment

Think about the poem. Then answer the questions. Fill in the circle next to the correct answer.

1. What "is never weary" in the poem?
   - (A) the poet
   - (B) the rain
   - (C) the wind
   - (D) the sun

2. What happens to the vine after the wind blows?
   - (A) Its leaves are blown off.
   - (B) It is blown from the wall.
   - (C) It gets soaked in the rain.
   - (D) The wall falls onto it.

3. "Mouldering" probably means
   - (A) smooth.
   - (B) gray-colored.
   - (C) pointed.
   - (D) crumbling.

4. This poem is mostly about
   - (A) a vine that is dying.
   - (B) a change of seasons.
   - (C) a sorrowful mood.
   - (D) a rainstorm.

5. You can conclude that the poet probably wrote this poem
   - (A) when he was feeling depressed.
   - (B) after hearing some particularly good news.
   - (C) to bring cheer to a friend.
   - (D) to explain why people are sometimes happy.

6. At the end of the poem, the poet seems to realize that
   - (A) he will always feel this way.
   - (B) his feelings are only temporary.
   - (C) his moods are affected by the weather.
   - (D) he is not really sad after all.

7. Longfellow is comparing two things in his poem "The Rainy Day." What is he comparing?

_____

_____

_____

8

Word Cards

What Is the Word?
Write the word here.

_____

What Does the Word Mean?
Write the meaning here.

_____
_____
_____
_____
_____
_____
_____

What Does the Word Stand For?
Draw a picture of it here.

How Can You Use the Word?
Write a sentence using the word here.

_____
_____
_____
_____
_____
_____
_____
_____
_____
_____

Name _____ Date _____

Word Wheel

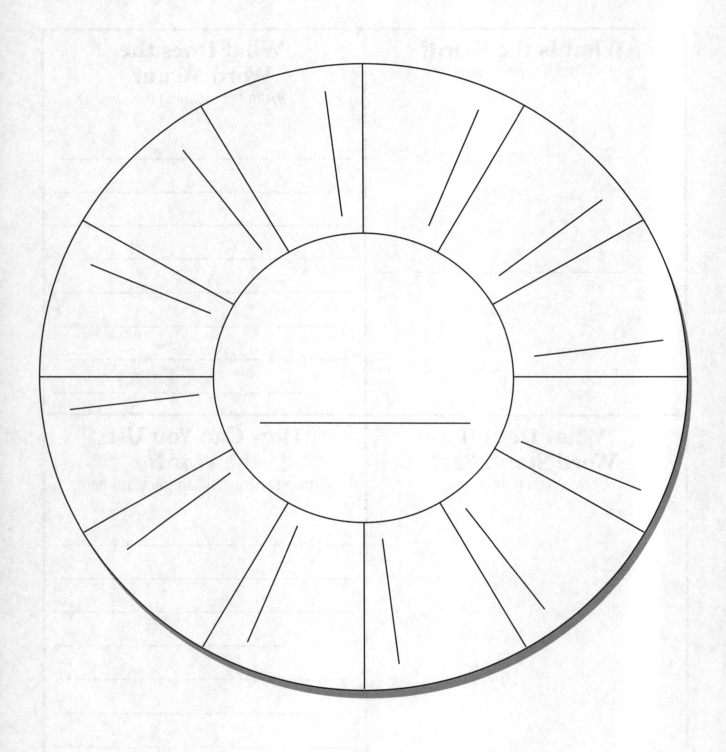

Resources: Word Wheel
Poetry: Grade 6, SV 9896-5

Graph

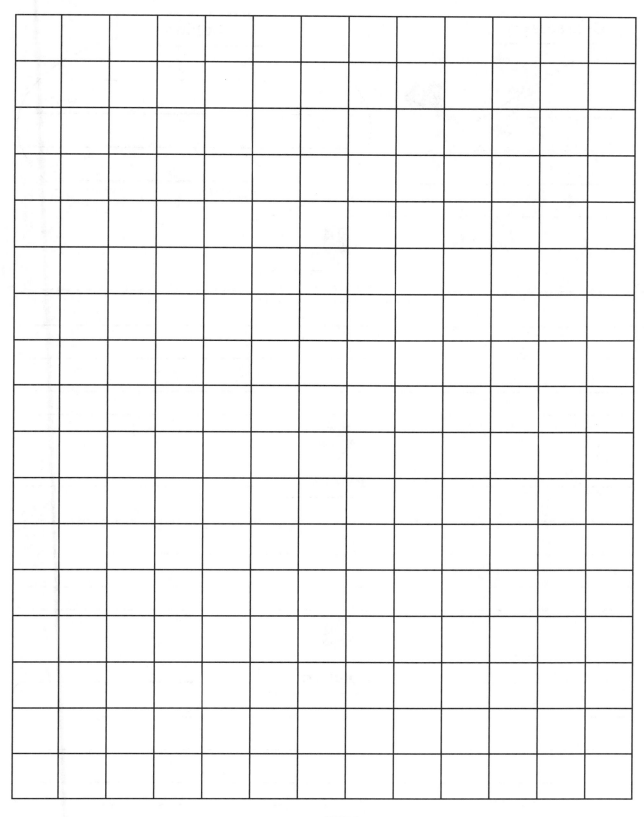

Name _____ Date _____

Story Map

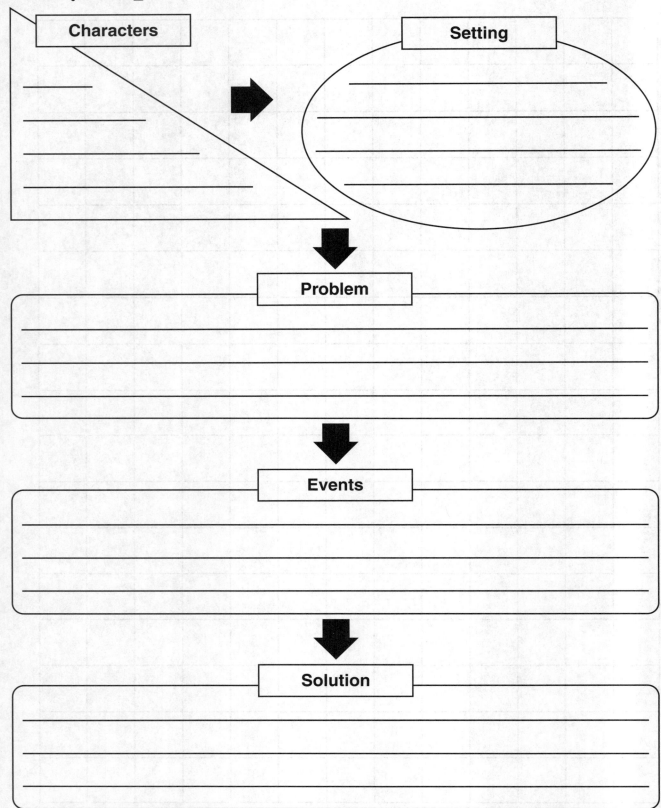

Characters

Setting

Problem

Events

Solution

Resources: Story Map
Poetry: Grade 6, SV 9896-5

Venn Diagram

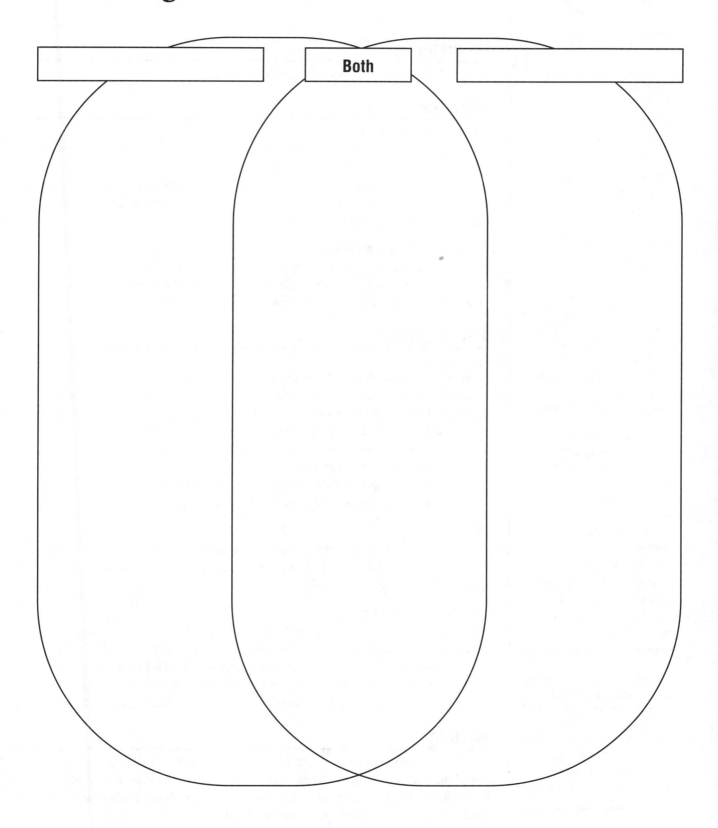

Both

LESSON 1

Pachycephalosaurus

Poetry Skill: Format

Standard
Identify and analyze the characteristics of fiction, nonfiction, poetry, and plays

Explore the Format of a Poem
Read aloud from a book or the Internet about the dinosaur Pachycephalosaurus. Then read the first verse from the poem. Lead students in a discussion to compare and contrast the poem and article formats. Explain that a poem is a snapshot of an idea or feeling.

Vocabulary

crease–to fold
jar–to move
knobs–bumps on the surfaces of things
nibbled–ate very little
projected–stuck out
protecting–keeping safe
proved–showed to be true
spikes–long, sharp pieces
worth–deserving

Teacher Tips

Point out to students that some poets make up words, like *kerwhacky*, to add humor or sound effects, or to draw attention to an idea.

Summary

The poet describes the head of a pachycephalosaurus.

Read the Poem

Introduce the Poem

Invite students to identify dinosaurs they find interesting. Challenge them to use specific adjectives to describe important features and characteristics. Then write *Pachycephalosaurus* on the board. Invite volunteers to read it and count the syllables. Ask students if they know anything about this dinosaur. Record students' responses.

Introduce the Vocabulary

Write the vocabulary words in any order on the board. Have partners alphabetize the words, find the definitions in a dictionary, and record the meanings, noting words that have more than one meaning.

After Reading

Questions

1. Why do you think that the poet says that the Pachycephalosaurus's brain is not worth protecting? (*It was a slow dinosaur that was not very smart.*)
2. What words does the poet use to describe the appearance or actions of the dinosaur? (*knobs, spikes, bump of bone, nibbled plants, bonehead*)
3. What does *bonehead* mean in contemporary language? (*stupid*)
4. What does the poet mean when he says, "To be a bonehead pays"? (*He is playing a game with words. Even though the dinosaur is a stupid "bonehead," the ten-inch bone in its head protects it.*)

Fluency

Explain to students that some poems have a specific rhythm, or beat. Then model how to read the first four lines with a steady cadence. Invite partners to practice reading rhythmically.

Develop Oral Language

Assign groups and have the students arrange their chairs in a circle. Explain that they will read the poem round-robin. Have students decide whether to read clockwise or counterclockwise. Then have one student read the first line. Without pausing in the poem's rhythm or cadence, the next person reads the second line. The reading continues with a new person reciting the next line.

Writing

Invite students to choose another dinosaur to write about. Using the word wheel on page 10, students write words that describe the appearance or most interesting characteristics of the dinosaur they chose. Then challenge students to write a paragraph or poem about the dinosaur.

Name _____   Date _____

Pachycephalosaurus
by Richard Armour

Among the later dinosaurs
Though not the largest, strongest,
PACHYCEPHALOSAURUS had
The name that was the longest.

Yet he had more than syllables,
As you may well suppose.
He had great knobs upon his cheeks
And spikes upon his nose.
Ten inches thick, atop his head,
A bump of bone projected.
By this his brain, though hardly worth
Protecting, was protected.

No claw or tooth, no tree that fell
Upon his head kerwhacky,
Could crack or crease or jar or scar
That stony part of Paky.

And so he nibbled plants in peace
And lived untroubled days.
Sometimes, in fact, as Paky proved,
To be a bonehead pays.

Name _____   Date _____

Pachycephalosaurus: Assessment

✎ **Think about the poem. Then answer the questions. Fill in the circle next to the correct answer.**

1. How was Pachycephalosaurus different from the other dinosaurs?
  Ⓐ It was the strongest.
  Ⓑ It had the largest body.
  Ⓒ It had the longest name.
  Ⓓ It had the smallest head.

2. If a tree fell on the head of a Pachycephalosaurus, it probably
  Ⓐ could not eat.
  Ⓑ didn't feel it.
  Ⓒ ran away.
  Ⓓ tore it up with its claws.

3. Which sentence below uses "projected" with the same meaning as in the lines of the poem?
  Ten inches thick, atop his head,
  A bump of bone projected.
  Ⓐ The senator projected a tax decrease.
  Ⓑ The cannon projected shells.
  Ⓒ Motion pictures are projected on a screen.
  Ⓓ The rocky point projected far into the water.

4. If this poem needed a new title, which would be the best one?
  Ⓐ "Later Dinosaurs"
  Ⓑ "A Bonehead with a Long Name"
  Ⓒ "Untroubled Days"
  Ⓓ "Knobs and Spikes"

5. Paky was able to nibble plants in peace because
  Ⓐ his brain was protected by a thick bone on top of his head.
  Ⓑ other dinosaurs feared him, so they left him alone.
  Ⓒ he was smarter than most of the other dinosaurs.
  Ⓓ the great knobs on Paky's cheeks protected his head.

6. What was the author's purpose in writing this poem?
  Ⓐ to inform readers about different kinds of dinosaurs
  Ⓑ to persuade readers that many dinosaurs were not dangerous
  Ⓒ to describe what different dinosaurs looked like
  Ⓓ to entertain readers with a lighthearted poem about a dinosaur

7. What is the mood of the poem? What does the poet do to capture this mood?

_____

_____

Name _____ Date _____

Homographs

Homographs are words that have the same spelling but different meanings. Use words in the sentence to help you choose the correct meaning of a word.

Example: watch
Meaning A: to look at
Meaning B: a tool that tells time

Read each sentence. What does the word in dark print mean? Write the letter for the meaning of the word.

knobs
Meaning A: bumps on surfaces
Meaning B: handles on doors and furniture

_____ **1.** Mrs. West replaced the **knobs** on all of her doors.

_____ **2.** It was easy to climb the mountain because of the many **knobs** that could be used as footholds.

spikes
Meaning A: long, sharp pieces
Meaning B: to swiftly hit a volleyball over the net and straight to the floor

_____ **3.** Marita **spikes** the ball, which helps her team score another point.

_____ **4.** Some knights wore **spikes** on their armor.

jar
Meaning A: to move
Meaning B: a container made of glass

_____ **5.** Small earthquakes often **jar** the dishes in the cabinets.

_____ **6.** There is tea in the **jar**.

crack
Meaning A: to break
Meaning B: a small, thin opening

_____ **7.** The child looked out through a **crack** in the door.

_____ **8.** A glass plate will **crack** if it falls on the floor.

The Bumblebee

Poetry Skill: Dialect

Standard
Identify the use of figurative language (simile, metaphor, personification, dialect)

Explore Dialect
Explain to students that dialect is a form of figurative language used to develop characters and enhance tone. Discuss the fact that people who live in the same area or share the same culture also share language habits. After sharing examples of dialect familiar to students, point out that poets try to show dialect by writing the way they hear people speak or using voiced and unvoiced sounds. Explain that the words may be misspelled or have missing letters. Have students look at the poem and highlight examples of dialect.

Vocabulary

drone—to make a continuous, low hum
fagged—dialect for "tired"
folks—people
slouchy—dialect for "drooping"
stinger—the part of a bee that is sharp and causes pain

Summary
Using a strong Southern dialect, the poet tells about the events that transpire when he grabs a bee.

Read the Poem

Introduce the Poem
Invite students to share encounters they have had with bees or other stinging insects. Invite them to listen as one poet recounts his adventures with a bee.

Introduce the Vocabulary
Write sentences on the board using the vocabulary words. Read the sentences and challenge students to guess the definitions. Discuss each answer, explaining how context can show if the guess is correct. After the definition is learned, discuss which words show dialect.

During Reading
Read the poem aloud to students.

After Reading

Questions
1. Why do you think the poet used the kind of words that he did? (*He was trying to create a mood by using dialect.*)
2. Who might the Raggedy Man be? Explain. (*Most likely answer: He is a friend or neighbor because he seems to have told the poet not to play with the bee in the past. NOTE: Actually, a raggedy man is a hired helper.*)
3. What do you think the poet learned from his experience? (*Don't touch bees!*)

Fluency
The dialect may cause students difficulty as they read. Suggest that students choose six lines of the poem to practice until they can smoothly recite them.

Develop Oral Language
Have students read the poem as if there is no dialect.

Writing
Explain that the dialect used by the poet is much like the computer dialect students often use when they e-mail friends. Challenge students to write a poem or paragraph using computer dialect.

The Bumblebee

by James Whitcomb Riley

You better not fool with a Bumblebee!—
Ef you don't think they can sting—you'll see!
They're lazy to look at, an' kind o' go
Buzzin' an' bummin' aroun' so slow,
An' ac' so slouchy an' all fagged out,
Danglin' their legs as they drone about
The hollyhawks 'at they can't climb in
'Ithout ist a-tumble-un out ag'in!
Wunst I watched one climb clean 'way
In a jimson-blossom, I did, one day,—
An' I ist grabbed it—an' nen let go—
An' "*Ooh-ooh! Honey! I told ye so!*"
Says The Raggedy Man; an' he ist run
An' pullt out the stinger, an' don't laugh none,
An' says: "They *has* be'n folks, I guess,
'At thought I wuz predjudust, more er less,—
Yit I still muntain 'at a Bumblebee
Wears out his welcome too quick fer me!"

The Bumblebee: Assessment

Think about the poem. Then answer the questions. Fill in the circle next to the correct answer.

1. What did the bumblebee do in the poem?
- Ⓐ It stung the Raggedy Man.
- Ⓑ It flew by the poet.
- Ⓒ It stung the poet.
- Ⓓ It spoke to the poet.

2. Before the poet grabbed the jimson-blossom,
- Ⓐ the Raggedy Man appeared.
- Ⓑ the poet wore out his welcome.
- Ⓒ the Raggedy Man laughed.
- Ⓓ the bumblebee seemed sleepy.

3. This poem is written in an old dialect. The Raggedy Man says, "They *has* be'n folks, I guess,/'At thought I wuz predjudust, more er less." He is saying, "There have been folks, I guess,/That thought I was prejudiced, more or less." What does "prejudiced" mean?
- Ⓐ unable to understand
- Ⓑ against something without reason
- Ⓒ without any hope
- Ⓓ not very smart

4. Which of these is the main idea of this poem?
- Ⓐ Bumblebees may look harmless, but their sting is painful.
- Ⓑ If you are stung by a bee, you should remove the stinger.
- Ⓒ The Raggedy Man is an expert on bumblebees.
- Ⓓ Bumblebees have trouble climbing on flowers.

5. You can conclude that
- Ⓐ the poet has been stung many times.
- Ⓑ the Raggedy Man is a kind man.
- Ⓒ bumblebees sting for no reason.
- Ⓓ the poet likes to pick flowers.

6. Bumblebees most likely
- Ⓐ sting people when they see them.
- Ⓑ sting when they see flowers.
- Ⓒ sting when they are threatened.
- Ⓓ sting when they are full.

7. What does the Raggedy Man mean when he says:
"Yit I still muntain 'at a Bumblebee
Wears out his welcome too quick fer me!"?

_____

_____

_____

Dialect Words

Explore More

Dialect is using words that are common to a region or a group of people living in a special culture. A writer can show dialect in several ways. The writer uses words that are special to the area. The writer also might misspell words to show how they are spoken. Finally, a writer might also use an apostrophe (') to show that one or more letters are missing in the word.

Examples: stoked = excited   fer = for   'at = that

Find the dialect word in each sentence. Write the meaning or correct spelling of each word below the sentence.

1. Dan was all fagged out after soccer practice.

_____

2. He was feeling slouchy.

_____

3. So Dan wuz walking home very slowly.

_____

4. He heard the drone of a bee go buzzin' by his head.

_____

5. 'Ithout thinking, Dan swatted the bee with his hand.

_____

6. The bee must have gotten kind o' angry.

_____

7. It began to chase Dan, an' nen he ran all the way home.

_____

8. Dan muntained that the bee wanted to sting him.

_____

The Quangle Wangle's Hat

Poetry Skill: Narrative Poem

Standard
Identify a narrative poem

Explore a Narrative Poem
Ask students to define *narrator*. After students explore the word, have them suggest what a narrative poem might be. Conclude by telling students that this kind of poem tells a story. It has a plot, characters, and setting. It has lyrics and stanzas and is often longer than most poems. Give examples of narrative poems, such as "The Night Before Christmas" and many of the Dr. Seuss stories.

Vocabulary

airy–spacious
charmingly–beautifully
corkscrew–twisted
creatures–animals
grant–allow
humbly–not proudly
luminous–glowing
plainer–clearer

Research Base

"All . . . students deserve a deep, rich immersion in poetry as part of their literacy learning." (*Guiding Readers and Writers: Grades 3–6, p. 421*)

Summary

Edward Lear, the master of nonsense, shares a tale about all sorts of creatures who nest in the hat of the mysterious Quangle Wangle Quee.

Read the Poem

Introduce the Poem

Read the first stanza of the poem. Then invite students to draw their interpretation of what the Quangle Wangle Quee looks like. Have students share their drawings. Tell them that the poet, Edward Lear, often wrote long poems that appealed to the imaginations of children. Then ask students to listen for the plot of the poem.

Introduce the Vocabulary

Use the graph on page 11 to make a word find puzzle, writing the words below the puzzle. Duplicate the activity page for students. Have partners find the words in the puzzle and the meanings in a dictionary. Ask them to write a sentence using each word.

During Reading

Read the poem aloud to students.

After Reading

Activity

Review the elements of a narrative poem. Then have students complete the story map on page 12 to identify the different elements.

Fluency

While "The Quangle Wangle's Hat" is a fun poem to read, the nonsense words may cause students to read haltingly. Suggest that they choose a stanza to rehearse to develop automaticity.

Develop Oral Language

Have partners retell the story in their own words.

Writing

Remind students that "The Quangle Wangle's Hat" is a narrative poem—it tells a story. Challenge them to extend the poem and tell about another creature that comes to live on the Quangle Wangle's hat. Encourage them to make up their own nonsense words to match the mood and humor of the poem. Have them draw a picture to go along with their poem.

The Quangle Wangle's Hat
by Edward Lear

I.
On the top of the Crumpetty Tree
    The Quangle Wangle sat,
But his face you could not see,
    On account of his Beaver Hat.
For his Hat was a hundred and two feet wide,
With ribbons and bibbons on every side
And bells, and buttons, and loops, and lace,
So that nobody ever could see the face
    Of the Quangle Wangle Quee.

II.
The Quangle Wangle said
    To himself on the Crumpetty Tree,—
"Jam; and jelly; and bread;
    Are the best of food for me!
But the longer I live on this Crumpetty Tree
The plainer than ever it seems to me
That very few people come this way
And that life on the whole is far from gay!"
    Said the Quangle Wangle Quee.

III.
But there came to the Crumpetty Tree,
    Mr. and Mrs. Canary;
And they said,— "Did ever you see
    Any spot so charmingly airy?
May we build a nest on your lovely Hat?
Mr. Quangle Wangle, grant us that!
O please let us come and build a nest
Of whatever material suits you best,
    Mr. Quangle Wangle Quee!"

IV.
And besides, to the Crumpetty Tree
    Came the Stork, the Duck, and the Owl;
The Snail, and the Bumble-Bee,
    The Frog, and the Fimble Fowl;
(The Fimble Fowl, with a corkscrew leg;)
And all of them said,— "We humbly beg,
We may build our homes on your lovely Hat,—
Mr. Quangle Wangle, grant us that!
    Mr. Quangle Wangle Quee!"

V.
And the Golden Grouse came there,
    And the Pobble who has no toes,—
And the small Olympian bear,—
    And the Dong with a luminous nose.
And the Blue Baboon, who played the Flute,—
And the Orient Calf from the Land of Tute,—
And the Attery Squash, and the Bisky Bat,—
All came and built on the lovely Hat
    Of the Quangle Wangle Quee.

VI.
And the Quangle Wangle said
    To himself on the Crumpetty Tree,—
"When all these creatures move
    What a wonderful noise there'll be!"
And at night by the light of the Mulberry Moon
They danced to the Flute of the Blue Baboon,
On the broad green leaves of the Crumpetty
  Tree,
And all were as happy as happy could be,
    With the Quangle Wangle Quee.

The Quangle Wangle's Hat: Assessment

Think about the poem. Then answer the questions. Fill in the circle next to the correct answer.

1. Why was the Quangle Wangle Quee unhappy?
   - Ⓐ because his hat was full of animals
   - Ⓑ because he did not like so much noise
   - Ⓒ because he could not find his hat
   - Ⓓ because he never saw anyone

2. What happened right after the creatures saw the hat?
   - Ⓐ They made a lot of noise.
   - Ⓑ They asked to build their homes in it.
   - Ⓒ They were frightened off by the Quangle Wangle Quee.
   - Ⓓ They climbed to the top of the Crumpetty Tree.

3. The creatures said, "We humbly beg,/We may build our homes on your lovely Hat." "Humbly" means
   - Ⓐ rudely.
   - Ⓑ quietly.
   - Ⓒ meekly.
   - Ⓓ bravely.

4. The author's purpose in writing this poem was most likely
   - Ⓐ to demonstrate the number of creatures that could live in one hat.
   - Ⓑ to explain how a Quangle Wangle Quee lives.
   - Ⓒ to describe the Quangle Wangle Quee's hat.
   - Ⓓ to entertain readers with a fun and silly poem.

5. You can conclude that
   - Ⓐ the Quangle Wangle Quee was much happier at the end of the poem.
   - Ⓑ the creatures were taking advantage of the Quangle Wangle Quee.
   - Ⓒ the Quangle Wangle Quee's hat was as full as it could be.
   - Ⓓ the creatures were discouraged to see so many others in the hat.

6. It seems safe to assume that
   - Ⓐ the Quangle Wangle Quee will not stay in the tree.
   - Ⓑ the Quangle Wangle Quee would never turn any creature away.
   - Ⓒ the creatures had no other place to build their homes.
   - Ⓓ a Crumpetty Tree is a rather small type of tree.

7. What clues tell you that this poem is make-believe? Use another sheet of paper to write your answer.

24

Name _____   Date _____

Synonyms

A synonym is a word that means the same or almost the same as another word.

Examples: start—begin   happy—glad

Read each sentence. Find a word in the box that means the same or almost the same as the word in dark print. Write the word on the line.

airy	amazement	charmingly	corkscrew	creatures
grant	large	luminous	plainer	silently

1. Neisha walked around the garden in the **glowing** moonlight. _____

2. She had asked the owner to **give** permission for her to visit at any time. _____

3. Neisha wanted to see what **animals** came out at night. _____

4. She decided to rest at a large and **spacious** gazebo. _____

5. The woodwork on the railing was **beautifully** done. _____

6. She sat **quietly** for several minutes. _____

7. Soon she saw a **big** raccoon walk toward a nearby pond. _____

8. It had a **twisted** tail. _____

9. To her **surprise**, four little raccoons walked behind. _____

10. To Neisha, it was **clearer** than ever that the five raccoons were a family. _____

LESSON 4

You Are Old, Father William

Poetry Skill: Repetition

Standard
Recognize the use of repetition

Explore Repetition
Repetition is a sound device in which sounds, words, or phrases are repeated to emphasize a point. As students read the poem, ask them why the poet might repeat the phrase *"You are old,"* said the youth.

Vocabulary

incessantly–without stopping
locks–hair
manage–to have the ability to do something
mentioned–told at an earlier time
sage–a wise man
suet–the fat around an animal's kidneys that is used to make candles
supple–easy to bend
uncommonly–in a way that is not common

Summary

In this Lewis Carroll poem, a boy wants to know how an old man can do such amazing feats usually attributed to a younger person.

Read the Poem

Introduce the Poem

Ask students at what age a person is old and what actions qualify a person as being old. Then tell them that Lewis Carroll, author of *Alice's Adventures in Wonderland*, wrote a poem about an old man. Ask them to think about the adventures Alice encountered and then predict what the old man in the poem might do. Invite students to listen to the poem to check their predictions.

Introduce the Vocabulary

Write the words on sentence strips, cut the letters apart, and put the letters in mixed order in an envelope that has the definition of the word. Challenge groups of students to unscramble the letters to spell the word. Have each group say a sentence with their word. If students get stumped, give hints, such as identifying the first letter, a prefix, or a rhyming word.

During Reading

Invite volunteers to read the poem.

After Reading

Questions

1. Why do you think the son is asking so many questions? (*Answers will vary.*)
2. A stereotype is "an opinion held by people based on an image often used to judge others." In the poem, the son has stereotypes about old people. What are the characteristics, or stereotypes, that the boy uses to judge that the man is old? (*white hair, fat, weak jaws*)
3. What are some stereotypes that you have? Do you think that the stereotypes are valid? Why or why not? (*Answers will vary.*)

Fluency

Explain to students that expression is the way that something is said. Point out that using expression when reading communicates the feeling of characters or the mood of the poem. Then have partners discuss how the characters in the poem might be feeling and read the poem with an expression that reflects those emotions.

Develop Oral Language

Have groups of three students read the poem aloud. One person is the narrator, one is the son, and one is Father William. Encourage them to read their lines as if they are the characters.

Read the Poem

You Are Old, Father William
by Lewis Carroll

"You are old, Father William," the young man said,
  "And your hair has become very white;
And yet you incessantly stand on your head—
  Do you think, at your age, it is right?"
"In my youth," Father William replied to his son,
  "I feared it would injure the brain;
But now that I'm perfectly sure I have none,
  Why, I do it again and again."

"You are old," said the youth, "as I mentioned before,
  And have grown most uncommonly fat;
Yet you turned a back-somersault in at the door—
  Pray, what is the reason of that?"
"In my youth," said the sage, as he shook his grey locks,
  "I kept all my limbs very supple
By the use of this ointment—one shilling the box—
  Allow me to sell you a couple."

"You are old," said the youth, "and your jaws are too weak
  For anything tougher than suet;
Yet you finished the goose, with the bones and the beak—
  Pray, how did you manage to do it?"
"In my youth," said his father, "I took to the law,
  And argued each case with my wife;
And the muscular strength, which it gave to my jaw,
  Has lasted the rest of my life."

"You are old," said the youth; "one would hardly suppose
  That your eye was as steady as ever;
Yet you balanced an eel on the end of your nose—
  What made you so awfully clever?"
"I have answered three questions, and that is enough,"
  Said his father; "don't give yourself airs!
Do you think I can listen all day to such stuff?
  Be off, or I'll kick you downstairs!"

You Are Old, Father William: Assessment

✒ **Think about the poem. Then answer the questions. Fill in the circle next to the correct answer.**

1. Who is asking Father William all the questions in the poem?
   - Ⓐ his grandson
   - Ⓑ his daughter
   - Ⓒ his father
   - Ⓓ his son

2. What does Father William threaten to do after he is asked the fourth question?
   - Ⓐ go to sleep
   - Ⓑ kick the person downstairs
   - Ⓒ stand on his head
   - Ⓓ eat a whole goose

3. What is the meaning of "supple" in the poem?
   - Ⓐ sturdy
   - Ⓑ thick
   - Ⓒ long
   - Ⓓ flexible

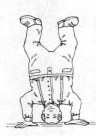

4. The purpose of this poem is to
   - Ⓐ describe what it is like to be elderly.
   - Ⓑ show how curious children can be.
   - Ⓒ entertain readers with a humorous conversation between two people.
   - Ⓓ warn children what can happen if they ask too many questions.

5. You can conclude that
   - Ⓐ Father William is quite lively for his age.
   - Ⓑ Father William does not like the boy.
   - Ⓒ the boy is afraid of Father William.
   - Ⓓ the boy has just met Father William.

6. The poet most likely believes
   - Ⓐ that standing on one's head can injure the brain.
   - Ⓑ that arguing can give one a strong jaw.
   - Ⓒ that children should be seen and not heard.
   - Ⓓ that poetry can be fun as well as serious.

7. What did the poet want people to learn by reading this poem?

   _____

   _____

   _____

   _____

Name _____   Date _____

Suffixes

A suffix is a small word part added to the end of a root word that changes the word's meaning.

Suffix	Meaning	Root Word	Example
able	able to be	manage	manageable
ful	full of	care	careful
less	without	help	helpless
ly	in a certain way	light	lightly

Read each sentence. Underline each word that has a suffix. Tell the meaning of the word. Use a dictionary if you need to.

1. Linda was cheerful as she walked with her grandfather.

Meaning: _____

2. The two talked incessantly as they went.

Meaning: _____

3. Linda asked endless questions about her grandfather's trips to China.

Meaning: _____

4. He patiently answered her.

Meaning: _____

5. Linda's grandfather was very knowledgeable about the country.

Meaning: _____

6. Linda was hopeful to visit China someday.

Meaning: _____

7. She asked so many questions because she was clueless about the people who lived in China.

Meaning: _____

A Misspelled Tail

Standard
Identify rhythm

Explore Rhythm
Explain to students that many poems have a specific rhythm, or repeated meter. Then read the first verse, overemphasizing the syllables to stress the beat. Then have partners read the poem, stressing the meter in each verse.

Vocabulary

awl–a tool that makes small holes in leather or wood
buoy–a water marker to signal a channel or danger
crewel–a kind of yarn
ewer–pitcher
fete–an expensive outside party
gneiss–a kind of rock like granite
heir–a person who will get money or things when someone dies
slay–to kill
sloe–a fruit from the blackthorn plant

Research Base

"To appreciate poetry is to appreciate the art of language." (*Guiding Readers and Writers: Grades 3–6*, p. 410)

Summary

Filled with homophones, the poem tells a story about a "buoy" who loses his "weigh" when he goes "four" a "slay" ride.

Read the Poem

Introduce the Poem

Ask students to write this sentence: *Maria wants to go to the park with her two brothers, too.* Ask students what is interesting about some of the words in the sentence. Guide them to notice the words *to, two,* and *too.* Explain that homophones are words that sound the same but have different spellings and meanings. Challenge partners to brainstorm a list of homophones.

Introduce the Vocabulary

Write the vocabulary words on the board and discuss their meanings. Point out that all the words are homophones. Invite students to make a crossword puzzle using the homophones of the vocabulary words as clues and the vocabulary words as the puzzle answers.

During Reading

Invite volunteers to read the poem.

After Reading

Questions

1. Was this poem hard to read or understand? Explain. (*Answers will vary.*)
2. What was the weather like when the poem started? (*clear and sunny*)
3. How did the weather change? (*It began to snow, sleet, and rain.*)
4. What different feelings did the boy experience during the poem? (*He was happy at first to go out on his sled. Then he got scared when he lost his way. Finally, he was relieved to be on his way back home.*)

Fluency

The homophones may cause students to read haltingly. Suggest they rewrite the poem using the correct spellings for each word's intended meaning before rehearsing the poem.

Develop Oral Language

Point out the "abab" rhyming pattern of the poem. Then divide the class in half. Assign one half of the class the "a" (first and third) rhyming lines of each verse to read and the other half the "b" (second and fourth) rhyming lines to read.

Writing

Challenge students to write a four-line poem using the homophones *to, two,* and *too.*

A Misspelled Tail
by Elizabeth T. Corbett

A little buoy said, "Mother, deer,
    May I go out too play?
The son is bright, the heir is clear,
    Owe, mother, don't say neigh!"

"Go fourth, my sun," the mother said.
    The ant said, "Take ewer slay,
Your gneiss knew sled, awl painted read,
    Butt dew knot lose your weigh."

"Ah, know," he cried, and sought the street
    With hart sew full of glee—
The whether changed—and snow and sleet,
    And reign, fell steadily.

Threw snowdrifts grate, threw watery pool,
    He flue with mite and mane—
Said he, "Though I wood walk by rule,
    I am not rite, 'tis plane.

"I'd like to meat sum kindly sole,
    For hear gnu dangers weight,
And yonder stairs a treacherous whole—
    Two sloe has been my gate.

"A peace of bred, a nice hot stake,
    I'd chews if I were home,
This crewel fete my hart will brake,
    Eye love knot thus to roam.

"I'm week and pail, I've mist my rode,"
    But here a carte came past,
He and his sled were safely toad
    Back two his home at last.

A Misspelled Tail: Assessment

Think about the poem. Then answer the questions. Fill in the circle next to the correct answer.

1. What did the boy in the poem take with him on his walk?
Ⓐ a deer
Ⓑ a plane
Ⓒ a sleigh
Ⓓ an ant

2. After the weather changed, the boy
Ⓐ got lost.
Ⓑ got scared.
Ⓒ ate steak.
Ⓓ went out to play.

3. Which of the following is a homophone for "gneiss"?
Ⓐ niece
Ⓑ nice
Ⓒ guess
Ⓓ geese

4. Another title for this poem could be
Ⓐ "Weight Fore Snow."
Ⓑ "Know Time Four Fun."
Ⓒ "A Son Day."
Ⓓ "Sum Slay Troubles."

5. When the poet returns home, he will most likely
Ⓐ sleep.
Ⓑ eat.
Ⓒ go out again.
Ⓓ watch TV.

6. You can infer that the poet
Ⓐ dislikes the snow.
Ⓑ will not go out in the snow ever again.
Ⓒ enjoys playing with words.
Ⓓ will watch the roads more closely.

7. Do you think the title is a good one for the poem? Why or why not?

_____

_____

Homophones

Explore More

Homophones are words that sound alike, but they have different spellings and meanings.

Example: Sam tried to **shoo** the bee away with his **shoe**.

shoe = something worn on the foot
shoo = to scare away

Read each sentence. Find each homophone that is used incorrectly. Underline it. Then rewrite the sentences using the correct homophones.

1. When I am board, I right poems.

_____

2. Keesha red a knew book of tall tails.

_____

3. No won is aloud two talk during a fire drill.

_____

4. Wear is ewer gnu slay?

_____

5. I can knot weight four the flours two grow.

_____

6. Wee are studying sells in hour science class.

_____

7. Due you no how too go two the library?

_____

8. The heir is gneiss and fresh today.

_____

O Captain! My Captain!

Summary

Walt Whitman tells of the successful voyage of a ship, though the captain has fallen dead.

Read the Poem

Introduce the Poem

Knowing additional information about a poem often helps the reader to understand the poem better. Whitman's poem was written soon after the American Civil War ended. Whitman had worked in a troop hospital during the war. Whitman was also a great admirer of President Abraham Lincoln. Lincoln was assassinated days before a peace treaty was signed to end the war. Share this information with the students, then have them read the poem.

Introduce the Vocabulary

Write sentences on the board using the vocabulary words. Read the sentences and challenge students to guess the definitions. Discuss each answer, explaining how context can show if the guess is correct. After the definition is learned, have students suggest other sentences using the word.

During Reading

Invite volunteers to read the different sections of the poem.

After Reading

Questions

1. What has happened to the captain in the poem? (*He has died.*)
2. Has the ship's voyage been successful? (*Yes, even though the captain has died.*)
3. The whole poem is a metaphor. What does Whitman seem to be comparing in his poem? (*He is comparing the end of a ship's voyage to the end of the Civil War, and the death of the captain to the death of Abraham Lincoln.*)
4. What are the "fearful trip" the poet mentions in line 1 and the "prize" in line 2? (*The fearful trip is the Civil War, and the prize is victory in the war.*)

Fluency

Point out that many poems have a rhythm, or beat. Then model how to read the poem rhythmically. Also point out the exclamation marks and model how to read these lines with emotion. Have students practice reading the poem to develop fluency.

Develop Oral Language

Have students use their own words to explain the poem.

Writing

Have students choose a sad event in their lives or a current event. Invite them to write a paragraph or poem about the event, and include a metaphor.

www.harcourtschoolsupply.com
© Harcourt Achieve Inc. All rights reserved.

34

Lesson 6 • O Captain! My Captain!: Teacher Information
Poetry: Grade 6, SV 9896-5

O Captain! My Captain!
by Walt Whitman

O Captain! my Captain! Our fearful trip is done,
The ship has weather'd every rack, the prize we sought is won,
The port is near, the bells I hear, the people all exulting,
While follow eyes the steady keel, the vessel grim and daring;
    But O heart! heart! heart!
     O the bleeding drops of red,
      Where on the deck my Captain lies,
       Fallen cold and dead.

O Captain! my Captain! rise up and hear the bells;
Rise up—for you the flag is flung—for you the bugle trills,
For you bouquets and ribbon'd wreaths—for you the shores a-crowding,
For you they call, the swaying mass, their eager faces turning;
    Here Captain! dear father!
     The arm beneath your head;
      It is some dream that on the deck,
       You've fallen cold and dead.

My Captain does not answer, his lips are pale and still,
My father does not feel my arm, he has no pulse nor will,
The ship is anchor'd safe and sound, its voyage closed and done,
From fearful trip the victor ship comes in with object won:
    Exult O shores, and ring O bells!
     But I, with mournful tread,
      Walk the deck my Captain lies,
       Fallen cold and dead.

O Captain! My Captain!: Assessment

Think about the poem. Then answer the questions. Fill in the circle next to the correct answer.

1. The Captain does not answer because
Ⓐ he does not know the answer.
Ⓑ he is dreaming.
Ⓒ he is busy sailing the ship.
Ⓓ he is cold and dead.

2. After the poet finds the captain dead,
Ⓐ he exults.
Ⓑ he walks the deck in sorrow.
Ⓒ he rings a bell.
Ⓓ he raises a flag.

3. Another word for "victor" is
Ⓐ loser.
Ⓑ swimmer.
Ⓒ captain.
Ⓓ winner.

4. This poem is mostly about
Ⓐ the sorrowful death of an admired man.
Ⓑ how to sail a ship correctly.
Ⓒ how crowds will cheer for anything.
Ⓓ how sea voyages can be dangerous.

5. You can conclude that the poet is upset because
Ⓐ he did not want the voyage to end.
Ⓑ the captain is dead.
Ⓒ the ship sank.
Ⓓ he is cold.

6. You can infer from the poem that
Ⓐ the poet was not a good sailor.
Ⓑ the poet is dead.
Ⓒ the poet is angry the trip is over.
Ⓓ the poet admired the captain.

7. Whitman's poem includes the emotions of joy and sadness. What words or lines show these emotions in the poem?

_____

_____

_____

www.harcourtschoolsupply.com
© Harcourt Achieve Inc. All rights reserved.

36

Lesson 6 • O Captain! My Captain!: Poem Assessment
Poetry: Grade 6, SV 9896-5

Name _____   Date _____

Antonyms

Antonyms are words with opposite meanings.
   Examples: open—closed   high—low   short—long

 Write the letter of the antonym beside each word.

_____	**1.** won	**A.** bored
_____	**2.** near	**B.** colorful
_____	**3.** eager	**C.** victor
_____	**4.** dead	**D.** happy
_____	**5.** fearful	**E.** endangered
_____	**6.** pale	**F.** lost
_____	**7.** mournful	**G.** alive
_____	**8.** exulting	**H.** distant
_____	**9.** loser	**I.** unafraid
_____	**10.** safe	**J.** weeping

Choose four pairs of antonyms. Write a sentence using each pair of antonyms.

11. _____

_____

12. _____

_____

13. _____

_____

14. _____

_____

www.harcourtschoolsupply.com
© Harcourt Achieve Inc. All rights reserved.

37

Lesson 6 • O Captain! My Captain!: Vocabulary Skill
Poetry: Grade 6, SV 9896-5

The Echoing Green

Summary

The poet describes a joyous day in the park.

Poetry Skill: Simile

Standard
Recognize the use of figurative language (simile, metaphor, personification, dialect)

Explore Similes
Explain to students that a simile is a poetic device in which two things that are not really alike are compared by using the words *like* or *as*. Then have students complete different similes, including *ran as fast as a _, hot as a _,* and *the children talked like _.* Challenge students to find the simile in the poem.

Vocabulary

descend–to move lower
folk–people
green–grassy land
sport–play
weary–tired

Read the Poem

Introduce the Poem
Have students brainstorm a list of things they do at a park. Then invite them to listen to a poem about a day in the park long ago.

Introduce the Vocabulary
Write the vocabulary words on the board. Have partners alphabetize the words, find the definitions in a dictionary, and record the meanings, noting words that have more than one meaning.

During Reading

Invite volunteers to read the poem.

After Reading

Questions
1. How long do the people spend on the green? (*from the time the sun rises to its setting*)
2. What do the older people in the poem think about? (*They think about playing on the green as young children.*)
3. Why do you think the poet calls the park the children play in "Echoing Green"? (*Possible answer: An echo is "a repeated sound." In the poem, lots of children through the years have repeatedly played on the green.*)

Fluency
The short lines, rhyme, and rhythm might cause students to read the poem quickly and without expression. Encourage the students to review the poem for times they may want to speed or slow the pace or change the tone of their voice to break the flow and add interest.

Develop Oral Language
Invite partners to alternate reading couplets.

Writing

Remind students that the older people in the poem think about the joys of youth as they watch the children play. Then ask them to think about a time in their past that was special to them. Challenge them to write a short verse using rhyming couplets about their "good old days."

The Echoing Green

by William Blake

The sun does arise,
And make happy the skies;
The merry bells ring
To welcome the Spring;
The skylark and thrush,
The birds of the bush,
Sing louder around,
To the bells' cheerful sound,
While our sports shall be seen,
On the Echoing Green.
Old John, with white hair,
Does laugh away care,
Sitting under the oak,
Among the old folk.
They laugh at our play,
And soon they all say:
"Such, such were the joys
When we all, girls and boys,
In our youth-time were seen,
On the Echoing Green."
Till the little ones, weary,
No more can be merry;
The sun does descend,
And our sports have an end.
Round the laps of their mothers,
Many sisters and brothers,
Like birds in their nest,
Are ready for rest,
And sport no more seen,
On the darkening Green.

The Echoing Green: Assessment

Think about the poem. Then answer the questions. Fill in the circle next to the correct answer.

1. What causes the children to stop playing?
   Ⓐ They are bored.
   Ⓑ They are tired.
   Ⓒ The old people laugh at them.
   Ⓓ The mothers tell them to come home.

2. What happens after the people laugh at the children playing?
   Ⓐ They think about the fun they had as children.
   Ⓑ They call the children to look at a nest.
   Ⓒ They ring the bell.
   Ⓓ Old John sits under a tree.

3. When the sun "descends," it
   Ⓐ rises.
   Ⓑ shines.
   Ⓒ sets.
   Ⓓ hides.

4. Which of the following is the BEST summary of the poem?
   Ⓐ The birds of spring sing along with the sound of cheerful bells.
   Ⓑ Old folks sit under a tree and think about their youth.
   Ⓒ Children play on the green from sunrise to sunset as old folks watch.
   Ⓓ Sleepy children go to their mothers as the sun goes down.

5. The poem is told from the point of view of
   Ⓐ one of the children.
   Ⓑ Old John.
   Ⓒ one of the parents.
   Ⓓ an unknown speaker.

6. The poet wishes to reflect which human experience in the poem?
   Ⓐ the hardships of old age
   Ⓑ the carefree joys of childhood
   Ⓒ regret for lost opportunities
   Ⓓ the uncertainty of life

7. What is the mood of the poem?

_____

_____

Homographs

Homographs are words that have the same spelling but different meanings. Use words in the sentence to help you choose the correct meaning of a word.

Example: bat
Meaning A: an animal that flies
Meaning B: something used to strike a ball

Read each sentence. Write a sentence using the underlined homograph with a new meaning. Use a dictionary if you need to.

1. The children played on the <u>green</u> grass.

   _____

2. Some children had fun playing the <u>sport</u> of baseball.

   _____

3. Other children made up a <u>play</u> to show their friends.

   _____

4. They even included a <u>folk</u> song in the show.

   _____

5. The <u>rest</u> of the children played on the playground.

   _____

6. The littlest <u>ones</u> played in the sandbox.

   _____

7. One girl found a toy <u>ring</u> in the sand.

   _____

8. She put it on her <u>hand</u>.

   _____

Piano

Poetry Skill: Rhyming Words

Standard
Identify rhyme

Explore Rhyming Words
The use of rhyming couplets will help students develop an understanding of rhyming words. Have students find the rhyming word pairs and highlight them using different colors. Help them identify the rhyming pattern. Then have students choose one of the word pairs and brainstorm other words that rhyme with it and write them on the word wheel on page 10.

Vocabulary

appassionato–musical directions to play with strong emotion or feeling
betrays–shows without intending to
cast–thrown
clamour–(clamor) a loud noise
insidious–not easily recognized
parlour–(parlor) family room
poised–balanced
vista–a mental picture

Summary

The poet hears a person singing, and it reminds him of a time when his mother played the piano and sang to him. Wishing for the past, he cries.

Read the Poem

Introduce the Poem

Gather an object that has special meaning for you and inspires a strong emotional response. During class, share the item and the emotion. Then have students draw a picture of something that when seen or heard, also makes them feel a certain way. Then ask students to listen to a poem about a piano and its meaning for the poet.

Introduce the Vocabulary

Write the vocabulary words and the definitions on separate cards. Pin them to a bulletin board. Say a sentence with a vocabulary word and ask a volunteer to find the word and the definition that matches. Discuss the word and definitions as needed.

During Reading

Ask volunteers to read the poem.

After Reading

Questions

1. What kind of mood does the poem have? (*sad*)
2. What caused the poet to feel sad? (*A woman who was singing and playing the piano made him think about his youth when he spent time with his mother.*)
3. Why do you think the poet wrote "Piano"? (*to share an emotional response that was important to him*)

Fluency

Discuss with students how this poem inspires a strong emotional response. Ask what the tone is and how someone should read the poem to reflect it. Have partners take turns reading the poem with the proper expression.

Develop Oral Language

Have students retell the poem in their own words.

Writing

Ask students to review their drawing of the object that made them feel strongly. Challenge them to write a brief poem that shares the emotion it causes and why.

Piano

by D. H. Lawrence

Softly, in the dusk, a woman is singing to me;
Taking me back down the vista of years, till I see
A child sitting under the piano, in the boom of the tinkling strings
And pressing the small, poised feet of a mother who smiles as she sings.

In spite of myself, the insidious mastery of song
Betrays me back, till the heart of me weeps to belong
To the old Sunday evenings at home, with winter outside
And hymns in the cozy parlour, the tinkling piano our guide.

So now it is vain for the singer to burst into clamour
With the great black piano appassionato. The glamour
Of childish days is upon me, my manhood is cast
Down in the flood of remembrance, I weep like a child for the past.

Piano: Assessment

✎ **Think about the poem. Then answer the questions. Fill in the circle next to the correct answer.**

1. Who is playing the piano in the poet's memory?
- Ⓐ a mother
- Ⓑ a sister
- Ⓒ a child
- Ⓓ a man

2. How does the poet organize the events in the poem?
- Ⓐ The poem moves back and forth between the past and the present.
- Ⓑ The poem is written in chronological order.
- Ⓒ The poem is set in the past.
- Ⓓ The poem takes place in the present.

3. Which words are synonyms?
- Ⓐ clamour, noise
- Ⓑ poised, happy
- Ⓒ weep, laugh
- Ⓓ insidious, noticed

4. What is the theme of this poem?
- Ⓐ appreciation of the piano as an instrument
- Ⓑ the universal language of music
- Ⓒ the loss of innocence
- Ⓓ fond memories of childhood

5. How does the poet feel about his childhood?
- Ⓐ He has a mixture of pleasant and unpleasant memories.
- Ⓑ He feels a longing for his childhood.
- Ⓒ He mostly has unpleasant memories.
- Ⓓ He does not remember much about being a child.

6. Which word best describes the poet in this poem?
- Ⓐ practical
- Ⓑ sentimental
- Ⓒ shallow
- Ⓓ forgiving

7. What is the main reason that the poet weeps?

_____

_____

_____

Name _____   Date _____

Word Puzzle

Read each sentence. Choose a word from the box that correctly completes each sentence. Write the word in the puzzle.

| appassionato | betrays | cast | clamour | insidious | parlour | vista | poised |

Across

3. The musician played the piano with deep feeling and _____ .
6. The man _____ the line of his fishing pole out into the water.
7. My mother dislikes the _____ music that some stores play in the background.
8. We like to watch television in the _____ .

Down

1. The loud _____ of the fire truck woke us up this morning.
2. The surprised look on Frank's face _____ the fact that he did not think he would get caught taking the cookies.
4. The baby bird stood on the edge of the nest and was _____ to fly away.
5. The fast violin music gave Tina a _____ of a train moving quickly through the night.

Opposites

Standard
Identify a diamante

Explore a Diamante
A diamante is a seven-line poem that compares opposite noun pairs. The first half of the poem describes the first word in the pair while the second half of the poem describes the other word. This poem is arranged in the shape of a diamond and follows a formula.
Line 1: one noun
Line 2: two adjectives that describe line 1
Line 3: three verbs that end in "ing" that describe line 1
Line 4: four nouns, first two refer to line 1 and the next two refer to line 7
Line 5: three verbs that end in "ing" that describe line 7
Line 6: two adjectives that describe line 7
Line 7: one noun that is the opposite of line 1

Vocabulary

exuberant–having high spirits
grumbling–complaining
prank–a playful trick
relaxing–resting
scheming–making plans that are tricky or harmful
straining–stretching to the limits
stressful–having strain

Summary

Two diamante poems show how poets can create an image in the reader's mind simply by comparing two opposite nouns.

Read the Poem

Introduce the Poem

Have students look at the poems. Ask them how the poems differ from other poems they have read. Discuss the shape of the poems as well as the formula of the words. Tell students these poems are called diamante poems.

Introduce the Vocabulary

Write the vocabulary words and the definitions on separate cards. Pin them to a bulletin board. Say a sentence with a vocabulary word and ask a volunteer to find the word and the definition that matches. Then have students think of the opposite of that vocabulary word. Write the opposite on a card and pin it next to the vocabulary word.

During Reading

Invite students to read the poems. Have the students highlight the opposite parts in two different colors.

After Reading

Activity

Have students choose one of the diamantes. Distribute two word wheels on page 10 to each student. Have students write one noun on each wheel and the corresponding words the poet uses to describe the noun. This will enable the students to see each topic as being separate and less confusing.

Fluency

Help students explore how to read poems with commas. Remind them that a comma signals the reader to pause briefly. Then have students practice reading the diamantes fluently.

Develop Oral Language

Have partners share stories of times they experienced one of the nouns being described.

Writing

Invite students to write a "Diamante for Two." Have each student write the first half of a diamante, stopping on the fourth line after the second noun. Then have partners exchange papers and complete each other's poem. Ask partners to discuss the completed poems.

Name _____   Date _____

Opposites
by Anonymous

Trick
nasty, sneaky
plotting, scheming, planning
prank, joke, reward, surprise
giving, sharing, enjoying
sweet, tasty
Treat

Work
stressful, tense
thinking, straining, grumbling
business, computer, game, park
relaxing, amusing, laughing
exuberant, carefree
Play

Name _____ Date _____

Opposites: Assessment

🖋 **Think about the poems. Then answer the questions. Fill in the circle next to the correct answer.**

1. In the first diamante, what does the poet compare a trick to?
 ⓐ a prank
 ⓑ a surprise
 ⓒ a business
 ⓓ a reward

2. What usually happens after people stop working?
 ⓐ They go to school.
 ⓑ They relax.
 ⓒ They grumble.
 ⓓ They go to a park.

3. Which words are antonyms?
 ⓐ plotting, scheming
 ⓑ joyful, exuberant
 ⓒ grumbling, laughing
 ⓓ reward, surprise

4. Another title for the two diamantes could be
 ⓐ "Trick or Treat."
 ⓑ "Work and Play."
 ⓒ "Feelings."
 ⓓ "What People Do."

5. You can conclude that the poet
 ⓐ likes to work.
 ⓑ likes to relax.
 ⓒ likes to play tricks.
 ⓓ likes to eat sour foods.

6. According to the first diamante, which is a treat that the poet might like?
 ⓐ ice cream
 ⓑ liver
 ⓒ pickles
 ⓓ milk

7. What is the purpose of writing a diamante?

_____

_____

_____

_____

Antonyms

Antonyms are words with opposite meanings.

Examples: big—small   long—short   up—down

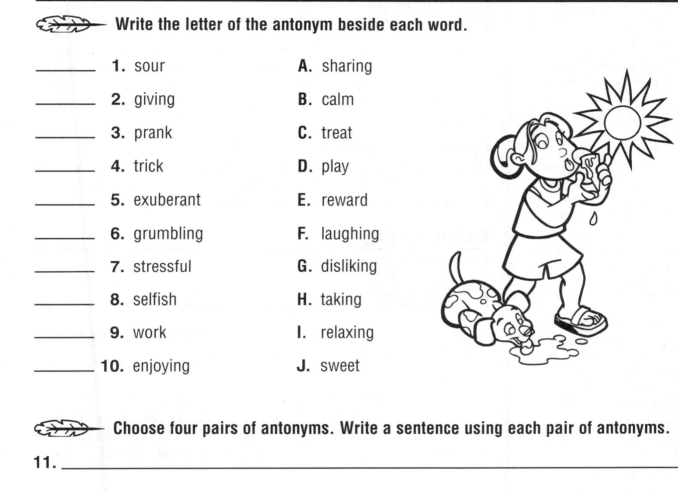

✎ **Write the letter of the antonym beside each word.**

_____ **1.** sour

_____ **2.** giving

_____ **3.** prank

_____ **4.** trick

_____ **5.** exuberant

_____ **6.** grumbling

_____ **7.** stressful

_____ **8.** selfish

_____ **9.** work

_____ **10.** enjoying

A. sharing

B. calm

C. treat

D. play

E. reward

F. laughing

G. disliking

H. taking

I. relaxing

J. sweet

✎ **Choose four pairs of antonyms. Write a sentence using each pair of antonyms.**

11. _____

_____

12. _____

_____

13. _____

_____

14. _____

_____

LESSON 10

The Open Window

Standard
Recognize the use of figurative language (simile, metaphor, personification, dialect)

Explore Personification
Explain to students that personification is a device in which human actions and ideas are given to things. Then discuss the examples in the first verse in which the house is given the human characteristic of standing and the light and shadow are playing. Challenge students to find the other example in the fourth verse.

Vocabulary

familiar–known through constant association
gravelled–covered with small stones
lindens–shade trees with heart-shaped leaves
playmates–friends
pressed–squeezed

Research Base

"**Poetry** is a microcosm for learning. Through the precise, concise language of poetry, students learn a lot about reading and writing." (*Guiding Readers and Writers: Grades 3–6, p. 421*)

Summary

A poet visits the house he grew up in and finds the house strangely quiet now that the children have all grown up and left.

Read the Poem

Introduce the Poem

Ask students how they feel when they look through photo albums and see themselves as young children. After they share their thoughts and emotions, invite students to listen to a poem about a poet who goes back to the house in which he grew up. Ask them to listen for the poet's feelings about the event.

Introduce the Vocabulary

Using the graph on page 11, make a word find puzzle. Write the words at the bottom of the page. After students find the words in the puzzle, have them find the definitions in a dictionary and record the meanings on the puzzle.

During Reading

Invite volunteers to read the poem.

After Reading

Activity

Distribute copies of the Venn diagram on page 13. Have students compare and contrast "The Open Window" to "Piano" on page 43.

Fluency

Explain to students that it is very important to watch for punctuation as they read so that they can understand the sentences in the poem. Model how to read the second verse by pausing for commas and reading line breaks smoothly. Then invite partners to practice reading the poem, being careful to watch punctuation.

Develop Oral Language

Have students explain the poem in their own words.

Writing

Review personification and the examples in the poem. Then ask students to write sentences that have personification and to draw pictures that correspond.

The Open Window
by Henry Wadsworth Longfellow

The old house by the lindens
    Stood silent in the shade,
And on the gravelled pathway
    The light and shadow played.

I saw the nursery windows
    Wide open to the air;
But the faces of the children,
    They were no longer there.

The large Newfoundland house-dog
    Was standing by the door;
He looked for his little playmates,
    Who would return no more.

They walked not under the lindens,
    They played not in the hall;
But shadow, and silence, and sadness
    Were hanging over all.

The birds sang in the branches,
    With sweet, familiar tone;
But the voices of the children
    Will be heard in dreams alone!

And the boy that walked beside me,
    He could not understand
Why closer in mine, ah! closer,
    I pressed his warm, soft hand!

The Open Window: Assessment

Think about the poem. Then answer the questions. Fill in the circle next to the correct answer.

1. What is standing by the door of the house?
- Ⓐ a woman
- Ⓑ a child
- Ⓒ a dog
- Ⓓ a tree

2. When did the poet squeeze the boy's hand?
- Ⓐ after he looked at the house
- Ⓑ after the boy squeezed the poet's hand
- Ⓒ before they got to the house
- Ⓓ before the boy went to play with the children

3. "Lindens" must be
- Ⓐ eaves.
- Ⓑ flowers.
- Ⓒ trees.
- Ⓓ mountains.

4. Which is the main idea of the poem?
- Ⓐ The poet is glad that the boy is with him.
- Ⓑ The house seems desolate with the children gone.
- Ⓒ The dog misses the children.
- Ⓓ The poet wishes that he had a house.

5. You can conclude that
- Ⓐ the poet knows why the children are gone.
- Ⓑ the poet has one of the children with him.
- Ⓒ the dog has been abandoned by the children.
- Ⓓ the children have run away from home.

6. What inference can you make from the tone of the poem?
- Ⓐ The poet does not care for children.
- Ⓑ The boy with the poet is afraid of the dog.
- Ⓒ The house they are looking at is haunted.
- Ⓓ The poet is sad the children are gone.

7. Why did the poet press the boy's hand?

_____

_____

Definitions

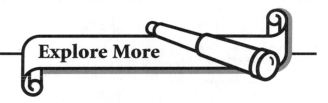
Explore More

Definitions are the meanings of words.

    Example: garden–ground used for growing fruits, vegetables, and flowers

Read each sentence. The words in dark print are the definitions. Find a word in the box that means the same as the words in dark print. Write the word on the line under the sentence.

| accepted | familiar | gravelled | inquired | lindens | playmates | pressed |

1. Ling called three of her **friends**.

_____

2. She **asked** if they would like to go on a picnic with her.

_____

3. Everyone **said yes to** the invitation.

_____

4. Once the friends arrived, Ling led them down the **stone** path.

_____

5. They set up a blanket under the **shade trees with heart-shaped flowers**.

_____

6. The friends had picnicked there when they were young children, so the place was **known** to them.

_____

7. To help them remember the day, the girls picked flowers and **squeezed** them between the pages of books to dry them.

_____

Ice

Poetry Skill: Metaphor

Standard
Identify the use of figurative language (simile, metaphor, personification, dialect)

Explore Metaphors
Explain to students that a metaphor is a poetic device in which two things that are unlike are compared so that one is said to be another. Metaphors do not use the words *like* or *as*. Then discuss the example, *Our dog was a fire-breathing dragon if anyone came near her puppies.* Challenge students to find the examples of metaphors in the poem.

Vocabulary

cruel–harsh
denied–not allowed
descended–moved down
endeavors–attempts
graceful–having or showing beauty
hosts–people who receive guests
wand–a magical stick
will–the power of the mind to decide something

Summary

The poet describes an ice storm.

Read the Poem

Introduce the Poem
Distribute the word wheel on page 10 and challenge partners to brainstorm words and images that describe an ice storm. After five minutes, gather the class and compile a master list on chart paper. Then invite students to listen to the author's description of an ice storm and see how many words or images from the poem match the list.

Introduce the Vocabulary
Write sentences on the board using the vocabulary words. Read the sentences and challenge students to guess the definitions. Discuss each answer, explaining how context would show that the guess was correct. After the definition is learned, have students suggest other sentences using the words.

During Reading

Invite volunteers to read the poem.

After Reading

Questions
1. Who does the poet blame for the icy weather? (*a fairy who makes a spell*)
2. What does the poet mean when she says, "And once proud trees did bow and bend"? (*The ice on the branches of the trees was so heavy that it made the trees bend low to the ground.*)
3. What does the poet think about the ice storm? How do you know? (*She thinks the iciness is beautiful, but that nature is cruel to cause so much destruction.*)

Fluency
Read aloud the first two verses of the poem in a steady, singsong rhythm. Point out that some poems have such a steady meter, causing the reader to read with little expression. Reread the verses, this time changing the pace and voice expression to add interest. Challenge partners to rehearse the poem several times to make the poem sound more varied.

Develop Oral Language
Invite students to do a dramatic reading of the poem and tape it on a cassette.

Writing

Remind students that the poet uses metaphors to describe the icy weather. Invite them to choose another kind of weather, write sentences with metaphors to describe it, and draw pictures to match.

Read the Poem

Ice
by Thomasin Heyworth

A frosty fairy's wand came down
And laid its spell upon our town
Of icy layers, cold and deep,
And then a watch did stay and keep.

All things existing and standing still
Were covered over by its will;
From blade of grass to buildings tall,
The ice chose not, but bathed it all.

The ice remained for days on end,
And once proud trees did bow and bend.
Their graceful branches once a crown,
Were laid upon the icy ground.

Its beauty could not be denied
Even as branches, heavy, cried,
And giving up dropped from their hosts,
And fell to earth as crashing ghosts.

The wires that brought us warmth and light
Were broken, useless, as the night
Descended bringing quiet dark,
Deep and complete but for candles' spark.

And I by candles' quiet light,
As breaking branches fill the night,
Describe a power, beautiful and cruel,
That makes man's endeavors seem those of fools.

             Poetry: Grade 6, SV 9896-5

Name _____   Date _____

Ice: Assessment

Think about the poem. Then answer the questions. Fill in the circle next to the correct answer.

1. What falls to earth in the poem?
Ⓐ trees
Ⓑ wires
Ⓒ branches
Ⓓ snow

2. When does the poet use a candle?
Ⓐ after the wires are broken
Ⓑ when the ice comes
Ⓒ before the storm
Ⓓ when the branches bend

3. "Endeavors" are
Ⓐ dreams.
Ⓑ attempts.
Ⓒ lives.
Ⓓ inventions.

4. Another title for this poem could be
Ⓐ "Bending Branches."
Ⓑ "A Cold Spell."
Ⓒ "Candlelight."
Ⓓ "Fixing the Wires."

5. You can conclude that
Ⓐ the ice is a powerful force of nature.
Ⓑ the poet's town is not equipped to handle storms.
Ⓒ the poet prefers candlelight to electric lamps.
Ⓓ the poet is afraid to have only candlelight.

6. This poem was most likely written
Ⓐ in 1900 during an ice storm.
Ⓑ by someone who was imagining an ice storm.
Ⓒ in modern times during an ice storm.
Ⓓ by a child who lived in the South.

7. What other problems might the poet face because of the ice storm?

_____

_____

_____

Dictionary Skills

Explore More

A dictionary tells how to say a word and what it means.

Look at the pronunciation key. Then circle the word that matches the pronunciation.

a	add	i	it	o͝o	took	oi	oil
ā	ace	ī	ice	o͞o	pool	ou	pout
â	care	o	odd	u	up	ng	ring
ä	palm	ō	open	û	burn	th	thin
e	end	ô	order	yo͞o	fuse	<s>th</s>	this
ē	equal					zh	vision

ə = { a in *above*   e in *sicken*   i in *possible*
      o in *melon*   u in *circus* }

1. (wond)   wound   won   wand

2. (hōsts)   hosts   hoists   whose

3. (kro͞o´ əl)   crawl   cruel   crew

4. (di send´ id)   designed   decided   descended

5. (in dev´ ûrz)   endeavors   indivisible   endears

6. (grās´ fəl)   grateful   graceful   grapple

7. (di nīd´)   denied   dented   dined

8. (kəm plēt´)   compliment   complicate   complete

Write the words that you circled above in alphabetical order.

9. _____

_____

LESSON 12

Snow in the Suburbs

Summary

The poet describes a snowy scene, including a bird that sets off an avalanche of snow and a thin black cat.

Poetry Skill: Assonance

Standard
Identify words that develop auditory skills, including alliteration, onomatopoeia, assonance, and consonance

Explore Assonance
Explain that assonance is a sound device in which similar vowel sounds are repeated in words, but they do not rhyme. Then read the first line of the poem: *Every branch big with it.* Explain that the short *i* sound is an example of assonance. Challenge students to find other examples of assonance in the poem.

Vocabulary

blanched–turned white
feeble–weak
inurns–buries
meandering–wandering
mute–quiet
nether–under
palings–fences made with thin, pointed boards
thrice–three times

Research Base

"**P**oetry is an essential, integral part of the language/literacy curriculum . . . ." (*Guiding Readers and Writers: Grades 3–6, p. 414*)

Read the Poem

Introduce the Poem

Invite students to share stories of their adventures in the snow. Then invite them to listen to one poet's story of snow.

Introduce the Vocabulary

Distribute eight word cards on page 9 to pairs of students. Ask partners to work together to complete a card for each word. Gather the students and ask different groups to discuss a word you name.

During Reading

Read the poem aloud to students.

After Reading

Questions

1. What are the suburbs? (*an outlying part of a city*)
2. What does the poet do to make the poem mimic the sequence of events set off by the bird? (*The rhythm of the words and the meter of the poem have a tempo that flow without pause, like snow falling off a tree. The poet also uses one long, run-on sentence to describe the event.*)
3. Where is the metaphor in the poem? What does the poet mean in the metaphor? ("The steps are a blanched slope." *The poet means the steps are covered with snow and look like the white slope of a mountain.*)

Fluency

Explain that expression is the way a poem is read. Then lead students in a discussion of the mood of the poem. Ask if the poet is excited or calm, happy or sad. Then read the poem several ways: fast and excited, slow and melancholy, and calm and happy. Have students tell which speed and voice reflect the mood of the poem. Point out how the words and images dictate the mood. Finally, have students practice reading the poem expressively.

Develop Oral Language

Assign groups and have the students arrange their chairs in a circle. Explain that they will read the poem round-robin. Have students decide whether to read clockwise or counterclockwise. Then have one student read the first line. Without pausing in the poem's rhythm or cadence, the next person reads the second line. The reading continues with a new person reciting the next line.

www.harcourtschoolsupply.com
58
Lesson 12 • Snow in the Suburbs: Teacher Information
Poetry: Grade 6, SV 9896-5

Name _____   Date _____

Snow in the Suburbs

by Thomas Hardy

Every branch big with it,
Bent every twig with it;
Every fork like a white web-foot;
Every street and pavement mute:
Some flakes have lost their way, and grope back upward, when
Meeting those meandering down they turn and descend again.
The palings are glued together like a wall,
And there is no waft of wind with the fleecy fall.
A sparrow enters the tree,
Whereon immediately
A snow-lump thrice his own slight size
Descends on him and showers head and eyes,
And overturns him,
And near inurns him,
And lights on a nether twig, when its brush
Starts off a volley of other lodging lumps with a rush.
The steps are a blanched slope,
Up which, with feeble hope,
A black cat comes, wide-eyed and thin;
And we take him in.

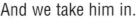

Name _____ Date _____

Snow in the Suburbs: Assessment

Think about the poem. Then answer the questions. Fill in the circle next to the correct answer.

1. The poet takes in
   Ⓐ a sparrow.
   Ⓑ a cat.
   Ⓒ a traveler.
   Ⓓ a bird.

2. After the bird lands in the tree,
   Ⓐ it flies away again.
   Ⓑ the cat frightens it.
   Ⓒ snow almost buries it.
   Ⓓ it finds a bug.

3. The black cat comes up the steps "with feeble hope." "Feeble" probably means
   Ⓐ weak.
   Ⓑ mistaken.
   Ⓒ old.
   Ⓓ lonely.

4. This poem is mostly about
   Ⓐ animals in the cold.
   Ⓑ a snowstorm.
   Ⓒ a bird in a tree.
   Ⓓ a hungry cat.

5. You can tell that
   Ⓐ the poet's family does not care for cats.
   Ⓑ the poet thought the bird was funny.
   Ⓒ the poet feeds the birds in the winter.
   Ⓓ the poet's family felt sorry for the cat.

6. It is likely that the poet
   Ⓐ has never seen snow.
   Ⓑ has many other cats.
   Ⓒ has a kind heart for animals.
   Ⓓ likes playing in the snow.

7. Why does the poet think the cat has feeble hope?

_____

_____

Synonyms

A synonym is a word that has the same, or almost the same, meaning as another word.
   Examples: small—little   happy—glad

Write the letter of the synonym beside each word.

_____	**1.** mute	**A.**	under
_____	**2.** meandering	**B.**	white
_____	**3.** inurns	**C.**	wooly
_____	**4.** nether	**D.**	weak
_____	**5.** descends	**E.**	quiet
_____	**6.** blanched	**F.**	breeze
_____	**7.** street	**G.**	road
_____	**8.** fleecy	**H.**	wandering
_____	**9.** waft	**I.**	drops
_____	**10.** feeble	**J.**	buries

 Use each vocabulary word in the box to write a sentence of your own.

palings	thrice

11. _____

_____

_____

LESSON 13

The Despot

Poetry Skill: Personification

Standard
Recognize the use of figurative language (simile, metaphor, personification, dialect)

Explore Personification
Explain to students that personification is a device in which human actions and ideas are given to things. Then discuss the examples: *The flowers nodded their lovely heads* and *The grandfather clock stood at attention, guarding the entrance of the house.* Challenge students to find examples of personification in the poem.

Vocabulary

appointed–in a set place
cowered–drew back in fear
decorously–in the proper manner
despot–an absolute ruler; a tyrant
devastating–causing destruction
elect–the chosen ones
hesitated–paused
reserved–quiet

Summary
A gardener decides the fate of the flowers that grow in a garden.

Read the Poem

Introduce the Poem
Lead students in a discussion of what a despot is and how one acts. Then discuss people in history who might be considered despots. Then read aloud the title of the poem. Ask students to listen to the poem to find out how the person being described is a despot.

Introduce the Vocabulary
Using the graph on page 11, make a word find puzzle. Write the words at the bottom of the page. After students find the words in the puzzle, have them find the definitions in a dictionary and record the meanings on the page.

During Reading
Read the poem aloud to students.

After Reading

Activity
Invite students to make a cartoon that tells the story's plot. Encourage them to be creative in their art, giving literal meanings to the figurative descriptions in the story. For example, students might draw a farmer who wears a crown on his head instead of a straw hat.

Fluency
Explain to students that commas and colons signal that a reader should pause briefly. Then model reading the third verse of the poem, pausing appropriately at each punctuation mark. Have students rehearse the poem to develop fluency reading different punctuation marks.

Develop Oral Language
Assign four students to each group and have them rehearse an oral presentation of the poem.

Writing
Ask students to choose other garden images. Have them write sentences in which the object is personified and then draw corresponding pictures.

Read the Poem

The Despot
by Edith Nesbit

The garden mould was damp and chill,
Winter had had his brutal will
Since over all the year's content
His devastating legions went.

Then Spring's bright banners came: there woke
Millions of little growing folk
Who thrilled to know the winter done,
Gave thanks, and strove towards the sun.

Not so the elect; reserved, and slow
To trust a stranger-sun and grow,
They hesitated, cowered and hid
Waiting to see what others did.

Yet even they, a little, grew,
Put out prim leaves to day and dew,
And lifted level formal heads
In their appointed garden beds.

The gardener came: he coldly loved
The flowers that lived as he approved,
That duly, decorously grew
As he, the despot, meant them to.

He saw the wildlings flower more brave
And bright than any cultured slave;
Yet, since he had not set them there,
He hated them for being fair.

So he uprooted, one by one
The free things that loved the sun,
The happy, eager, fruitful seeds
That had not known that they were weeds.

Understand the Poem

The Despot: Assessment

✎ **Think about the poem. Then answer the questions. Fill in the circle next to the correct answer.**

1. What did the gardener uproot?
   Ⓐ the flowers he planted
   Ⓑ the prettiest flowers
   Ⓒ the weeds
   Ⓓ the winter plants

2. The plants started to grow
   Ⓐ after winter.
   Ⓑ after the sun came out.
   Ⓒ after spring.
   Ⓓ after the dew.

3. What kind of person is a "despot"?
   Ⓐ a farmer
   Ⓑ a ruler
   Ⓒ a friend
   Ⓓ a soldier

4. The poem is mostly about
   Ⓐ flowers that grow all year long.
   Ⓑ planting seeds.
   Ⓒ choosing plants for a garden.
   Ⓓ a gardener who does not like weeds.

5. The "elect" were
   Ⓐ the flowers that the gardener planted.
   Ⓑ the wildflowers.
   Ⓒ the first flowers to grow.
   Ⓓ the sick flowers.

6. Most likely, the gardener
   Ⓐ didn't like to garden.
   Ⓑ was hired to care for the garden.
   Ⓒ liked only beautiful flowers.
   Ⓓ worked only in the spring.

7. How did the gardener feel about the weeds?

_____

_____

_____

_____

     Poetry: Grade 6, SV 9896-5

Classifying

Think about how word meanings are similar. Doing so can help you better understand what you are reading.

 Read each group of words. Cross out the word that does not belong.

1. damaging   devastating   destroying   depending

2. elected   voted   chosen   selected

3. ignored   hesitated   paused   halted

4. despot   monarch   ruler   friend

5. quiet   reserved   talkative   silent

6. gardeners   legions   soldiers   fighters

7. fair   cowered   beautiful   pretty

8. mannerly   well-behaved   decorously   actively

9. eager   cultured   interested   willing

10. prim   appointed   assigned   placed

Choose three word groups. Write a sentence using two of the words from each group.

11. _____

_____

12. _____

_____

13. _____

_____

Lesson 13 • **The Despot:** Vocabulary Skill
Poetry: Grade 6, SV 9896-5

Basho's Haiku

Summary

Basho, a seventeenth-century Japanese poet, wrote many haiku that told about his travels and his perspective on nature.

Read the Poem

Introduce the Poems

In advance, research Matsuo Basho, a Japanese poet who mastered the art of the haiku. Share the information with the students. Then tell them they will read three examples of Basho's haiku. Explain that the haiku are translations from the Japanese language and that different editors do not always interpret one poem with the same wording or even use the same punctuation. However, the meaning, emotion, and content are usually the same.

Introduce the Vocabulary

Write the vocabulary words on the board. Pair students and have them look up the words in the dictionary. Have them write down all the meanings of the words. Gather the students and discuss the words.

During Reading

Ask volunteers to read the haiku.

After Reading

Activity

Ask students to choose one of the haiku and draw a picture of it. Challenge them to capture the mood of the poem as well as the image. Then pair students and have them use the Venn diagram on page 13 to compare their poem pictures.

Fluency

Point out to students that although haiku are alike in the fact that they are observations of nature, each one can have a different mood or feeling to it. This can affect the way it is read aloud. Discuss the mood of each poem and challenge students to read each with the proper expression.

Develop Oral Language

Challenge students to memorize one of the haiku and share it with the class.

Writing

Have students think of a scene in nature and imagine that they are taking a picture. Have them use the word wheel on page 10 to organize the sights, sounds, colors, and actions that they associate with their nature topic. Challenge students to use the images to write their own haiku. Then have them draw a corresponding picture.

Poetry Skill: Haiku

Standard
Identify a haiku poem

Explore a Haiku Poem
Write one of the haiku poems on the board. Explain that a haiku is a kind of formula poem that originated in Japan. It focuses on one specific image, often from nature, that sets a mood or emotion. A haiku has three lines and a total of 17 syllables, often distributed in a specific 5–7–5 pattern:
Line 1: 5 syllables
Line 2: 7 syllables
Line 3: 5 syllables
Help students count the syllables of the poems.

Vocabulary

orchid–a kind of flower with a strong smell
perfumes–gives a sweet smell to
slants–has a slope
vast–large and wide

Basho's Haiku
by Matsuo Basho

Lady butterfly
perfumes wings by floating
over the orchid.

Moonlight slants through
the vast bamboo grove:
A cuckoo cries.

The old pond, yes, and
a frog is jumping into
the water, and splash.

Name _____ Date _____

Basho's Haiku:
Assessment

Think about the poems. Then answer the questions. Fill in the circle next to the correct answer.

1. In the second haiku, what is in the bamboo?
   Ⓐ a frog
   Ⓑ a butterfly
   Ⓒ a cuckoo
   Ⓓ a pond

2. After the frog jumps into the water, it makes a
   Ⓐ ripple.
   Ⓑ splash.
   Ⓒ drip.
   Ⓓ cry.

3. The word "slants" in the second haiku most likely means
   Ⓐ at an angle.
   Ⓑ a different way to view something.
   Ⓒ shining light.
   Ⓓ shadows.

4. A good title for the first poem would be
   Ⓐ "The Butterfly and the Orchid."
   Ⓑ "The Purple Butterfly."
   Ⓒ "Smelly Wings."
   Ⓓ "Sweet Smells."

5. You can conclude that an orchid
   Ⓐ is always purple.
   Ⓑ is a favorite flower of butterflies.
   Ⓒ floats on water.
   Ⓓ has a strong, sweet smell.

6. It would seem that the poet
   Ⓐ has a garden.
   Ⓑ makes observations about nature.
   Ⓒ likes frogs.
   Ⓓ grows bamboo.

7. Which is your favorite haiku? Why?

_____

_____

Homographs

Homographs are words that have the same spelling but different meanings. Use words in the sentence to help you choose the correct meaning of a word.

Example: water
Meaning A: liquid
Meaning B: to give liquid to living things

Read each sentence. What does the word in dark print mean? Write the letter for the meaning of the word.

perfumes
Meaning A: gives a sweet smell to
Meaning B: liquids that have sweet smells

_____ **1.** The store sold many kinds of **perfumes**.

_____ **2.** The scent of the flower **perfumes** the air.

orchid
Meaning A: a kind of flower with a strong smell
Meaning B: a deep purple

_____ **3.** Lisa bought an **orchid** blouse to match her lavender skirt.

_____ **4.** Mr. Ramos grows a special kind of **orchid** in his garden.

vast
Meaning A: large and wide
Meaning B: boundless space

_____ **5.** Chau's knowledge about butterflies was **vast**.

_____ **6.** Astronauts travel into the **vast** of the solar system.

slants
Meaning A: has a slope
Meaning B: biased views

_____ **7.** Many editorials in the newspaper have **slants** that give strong opinions.

_____ **8.** A roof **slants** to keep the rain from sitting on it.

LESSON 15

The Tables Turned

Poetry Skill: Rhyming Words

Standard
Identify rhyme

Explore Rhyming Words
Remind students that some poems use rhyming words. Then have students find the rhyming word pairs and highlight them using two different colors in each verse. Challenge students to find the rhyming pattern. Then have them choose one of the rhyming sets and write other rhyming words on the word wheel found on page 10.

Vocabulary

blithe–cheerful
leaves–pages in a book
lore–facts and stories about a specific topic
lustre–(luster) a bright, shiny surface
meddling–busying oneself in another person's life
mellow–soft, rich, and full
sages–wise and knowledgeable people
strife–argument
toil–work
vernal–spring

Summary

The poet implores his friend to put aside books and to learn from nature.

Read the Poem

Introduce the Poem
Ask students how they learn things. Record the responses on the board. Then have students listen to a poem about one poet's opinion of the best kind of teacher.

Introduce the Vocabulary
Write the vocabulary words on index cards, making enough so that each student gets one. Then distribute a word card activity on page 9 and an index card to each student. Have the students complete a card for their word. Then ask students having the same assigned word to meet to discuss their word. They can present what their word means to the rest of the class.

During Reading

Read the poem aloud to students.

After Reading

Questions
1. What is the poet's purpose in writing the poem? (*to convince the reader to go outside to view, experience, and learn from nature*)
2. How does the poet feel about books? (*He does not think they are useful.*)
3. What is the mood of the poem? (*humorous and exuberant*)
4. Why did the poet choose the title he did? (*Sample response: Most people think that reading books produces the most knowledge and is the best way to learn. The poet has a different point of view, thinking that people can learn more from nature, as well as get healthy as they move around outside.*)

Fluency
Point out the exclamation marks in the middle of sentences and explain that they indicate excitement. Discuss how someone would read those words. Have partners take turns reading verses that have exclamation points.

Writing

Review why the poet wrote the poem: to convince the reader to go out and learn from nature. Ask students to think of something they would like to convince someone to do. Invite them to write a paragraph or short poem to voice their opinion. Challenge students to include rhyming words in their writing.

Name _____   Date _____

The Tables Turned
by William Wordsworth

Up! up! my Friend, and quit your books;
Or surely you'll grow double:
Up! up! my Friend, and clear your looks;
Why all this toil and trouble?

The sun, above the mountain's head,
A freshening lustre mellow
Through all the long green fields has spread,
His first sweet evening yellow.

Books! 'tis a dull and endless strife:
Come, hear the woodland linnet,
How sweet his music! on my life,
There's more of wisdom in it.

And hark! how blithe the throstle sings!
He, too, is no mean preacher:
Come forth into the light of things,
Let Nature be your teacher.

She has a world of ready wealth,
Our minds and hearts to bless—
Spontaneous wisdom breathed by health,
Truth breathed by cheerfulness.

One impulse from a vernal wood
May teach you more of man,
Of moral evil and of good,
Than all the sages can.

Sweet is the lore which Nature brings;
Our meddling intellect
Mis-shapes the beauteous forms of things:—
We murder to dissect.

Enough of Science and of Art;
Close up those barren leaves;
Come forth, and bring with you a heart
That watches and receives.

Name _____   Date _____

The Tables Turned: Assessment

Think about the poem. Then answer the questions. Fill in the circle next to the correct answer.

1. What does the poet want his friend to do?
   Ⓐ to read with him
   Ⓑ to go outside
   Ⓒ to quit school
   Ⓓ to read to him

2. The poet suggests that after too many hours looking through books,
   Ⓐ a person may grow bent over double.
   Ⓑ a person will become very intelligent.
   Ⓒ a person will forget his or her friends.
   Ⓓ a person may be misinformed.

3. "Sages" are
   Ⓐ good books.
   Ⓑ wild animals.
   Ⓒ true friends.
   Ⓓ wise people.

4. The main idea of this poem is that
   Ⓐ people should live in the wild.
   Ⓑ there is no learning like the experience of nature.
   Ⓒ books have nothing to offer.
   Ⓓ reading is an unhealthy habit.

5. You can tell that
   Ⓐ the poet loves the natural world.
   Ⓑ the poet has never read a book.
   Ⓒ the poet cannot read.
   Ⓓ the poet does not go outside often.

6. Given the choice of an indoor or an outdoor pursuit, the poet would most likely
   Ⓐ take some time to make his decision.
   Ⓑ choose the indoor pursuit, but sit near a window.
   Ⓒ try to do both things at once.
   Ⓓ choose the outdoor pursuit without hesitation.

7. Why is nature a good teacher at times?

_____

_____

_____

Name _____   Date _____

Hink Pinks

Hink pinks are two or more words beside each other that rhyme. You can use hink pinks to solve riddles.

Example:
Riddle: What do you call arguments and hardship in life?
Hink pink answer: life strife

Read each riddle. Answer it with a hink pink. (Hint: Think about the words in dark print.)

1. What do you call work that is done in the **soil**?

s   o   i   l   ___ ___ ___ ___

2. What do you call **wages** that knowledgeable people are paid?

___ ___ ___ ___   w   a   g   e   s

3. What kind of **meddling** does a parent do when teaching a child to ride a bike?

___ ___ ___ ___ ___ ___ ___ ___

m   e   d   d   l   i   n   g

4. What kind of man is **mellow**?

a   m   e   l   l   o   w

___ ___ ___ ___ ___ ___

5. What kinds of **thieves** steal pages from a book?

___ ___ ___ ___ ___ ___ ___

t   h   i   e   v   e   s

6. What kind of **store** sells stories only about the beach?

a   ___ ___ ___ ___ ___   ___ ___ ___ ___ ___

s   t   o   r   e

Lesson 15 • **The Tables Turned:** Vocabulary Skill
Poetry: Grade 6, SV 9896-5

[from] The Pied Piper of Hamelin

Summary

In this excerpt, Robert Browning shares the story of the piper who rids a city of its rat problem.

Read the Poem

Introduce the Poem

Read aloud the Grimm Brothers' tale of the Pied Piper of Hamelin. Explain that the folk tale is believed to be based on a true event that took place in 1284 in Hamelin, Germany. Explain that there are many theories about what happened to the children, including being led out of town because they were diseased. Then invite students to listen to another writer's interpretation of the event.

Introduce the Vocabulary

Write the vocabulary words and the definitions on separate cards. Pin them to a bulletin board. Say a sentence with a vocabulary word and ask a volunteer to find the word and the definition that matches. Discuss the meanings.

During Reading

Ask volunteers to read the poem.

After Reading

Activity

Review the elements of a narrative poem. Then have students complete the story map on page 12 to identify the different elements.

Fluency

"The Pied Piper of Hamelin" uses words that may be unfamiliar to students and cause them to read haltingly. Ask them to highlight challenging words. Help students read the words and encourage them to practice them to develop automaticity.

Develop Oral Language

Have partners retell the story in their own words.

Writing

Remind students that they have read only a part of "The Pied Piper of Hamelin." Encourage them to find and read the entire poem, either on the Internet or in a book. Have them write a paragraph telling how they feel about the event and what lesson they learned.

Poetry Skill: Narrative Poem

Standard
Identify a narrative poem

Explore a Narrative Poem
Write *narrative* on the board and ask students to find the root from which the word is derived. Discuss its meaning and brainstorm other words derived from *narrate*, recording them on the board. After students explore the words, have them suggest what a narrative poem might be. Conclude by telling students that this kind of poem tells a story. It has a plot, characters, and setting. It is often longer than most other poems. Give examples of narrative poems, such as "The Night Before Christmas" and many of the Dr. Seuss stories.

Vocabulary

adept–very skillful
brawny–muscular
cherished–loved
commentary–a record of an event
drysaltery–a store that salted foods so they would not spoil
perished–died
plodders–people who walk slowly but steadily
shrill–high and sharp

Name _____ Date _____

[from] The Pied Piper of Hamelin
by Robert Browning

Into the street the Piper stept,
    Smiling first a little smile,
As if he knew what magic slept
    In his quiet pipe the while;
Then, like a musical adept,
To blow the pipe his lips he wrinkled,
And green and blue his sharp eyes
  twinkled,
Like a candle-flame where salt is sprinkled;
And ere three shrill notes the pipe uttered,
You heard as if an army muttered;
And the muttering grew to a grumbling
And the grumbling grew to a mighty
  rumbling;
And out of the houses the rats came
  tumbling.
Great rats, small rats, lean rats, brawny
  rats,
Grave old plodders, gay young friskers,
    Fathers, mothers, uncles, cousins,
Cocking tails and pricking whiskers,
    Families by the tens and dozens,
Brothers, sisters, husbands, wives,
Followed the Piper for their lives.
From street to street he piped advancing,
And step by step they followed dancing,
Until they came to the river Weser,
Wherein all plunged and perished!
—Save one, who, stout as Julius Caesar,
Swam across and lived to carry
(As he, the manuscript he cherished)
to Rat-land home his commentary:

Which was, "At the first shrill notes of the
  pipe,
I heard a sound as of scraping tripe,
And putting apples, wondrous ripe,
Into a cider-press's gripe,
And a moving away of pickle tub-boards,
And a leaving ajar of conserve-cupboards,
And a drawing the corks of train-oil-flasks,
And a breaking the hoops of butter-casks:
And it seemed as if a voice
(Sweeter far than by harp of psaltery
Is breathed) called out, 'Oh rats, rejoice!
The world is grown to one vast drysaltery!
So munch on, crunch on, take your
  nuncheon,
Breakfast, supper, dinner, luncheon!'
And just as a bulky sugar-puncheon,
All ready staved, like a great Sun shone,
Glorious scarce an inch before me,
Just as methought it said, 'Come,
  bore me!'
—I found the Weser rolling
  o'er me."

Name _____ Date _____

[from] The Pied Piper of Hamelin: Assessment

Think about the poem. Then answer the questions. Fill in the circle next to the correct answer.

1. What did the Pied Piper do to make the rats follow?
   Ⓐ He sang a song.
   Ⓑ He spoke a magic spell.
   Ⓒ He played a tune.
   Ⓓ He carried food.

2. Before the rats went into the river,
   Ⓐ the piper went into the river.
   Ⓑ they heard the sounds of food bins opening.
   Ⓒ they figured out what was happening.
   Ⓓ they ran back into the town.

3. "Perished" means
   Ⓐ swam.
   Ⓑ squeaked.
   Ⓒ sank.
   Ⓓ died.

4. This portion of "The Pied Piper" tells mostly about
   Ⓐ how the piper led the rats to the river.
   Ⓑ how the people of the village found the piper.
   Ⓒ what gave the piper his ability to lead the rats.
   Ⓓ how one rat made it across the river.

5. The rats appear
   Ⓐ to love to swim.
   Ⓑ to have been friends with the piper.
   Ⓒ to love food above everything else.
   Ⓓ to love music.

6. The story of the piper is most likely not
   Ⓐ based on a true story.
   Ⓑ an autobiography.
   Ⓒ based on a folk tale.
   Ⓓ a narrative poem.

7. The poem has two storytellers. Who are they? In what part of the poem does the view change?

_____

_____

_____

Name _____   Date _____

Antonyms

Antonyms are words with opposite meanings.
    Examples: big—small   long—short   up—down

 Write the letter of the antonym beside each word.

_____ **1.** adept   **A.** friskers

_____ **2.** shrill   **B.** lived

_____ **3.** plodders   **C.** hated

_____ **4.** brawny   **D.** unskilled

_____ **5.** plunged   **E.** retreating

_____ **6.** advancing   **F.** smooth

_____ **7.** perished   **G.** arose

_____ **8.** wrinkled   **H.** horrible

_____ **9.** cherished   **I.** bass

_____ **10.** glorious   **J.** skinny

 Write a sentence using each vocabulary word in the box.

> commentary   drysaltery

11. _____

_____

_____

LESSON 17

[from] **Paul Revere's Ride**

Standard
Identify a ballad

Explore Ballads
Explain to students that ballads are stories about famous people or events. Point out that a ballad has a plot, and the stanzas are arranged in chronological order so that the story unfolds in a logical sequence. As the students read the poem, discuss the chronological order that Longfellow presented by creating a story map on the board to record the poem's plot.

Vocabulary

grenadiers–a group of the best soldiers
magnified–made larger
moorings–places where boats or ships are tied
muffled–wrapped in something to deaden the sound
muster–to gather soldiers
phantom–a ghostly shape
sombre–(somber) dark and gloomy
stealthy–done in secret

Summary

In this ballad, Longfellow retells the story of Paul Revere's ride to warn of the British invasion.

Read the Poem

Introduce the Poem
Ask students what they know about Paul Revere and his claim to fame in the American Revolution. Then explain that the poet Henry Wadsworth Longfellow wrote a ballad telling about the event. Remind students that since the ballad is a long poem that tells a story, they will read only an excerpt of it.

Introduce the Vocabulary
Write sentences on the board using the vocabulary words. Read the sentences and challenge students to guess the definitions. Discuss each answer, explaining how context would show that the guess was correct. After the definition is learned, have students suggest other sentences using the words.

During Reading

Invite volunteers to read the poem.

After Reading

Activity
Remind students that they have read only a part of "Paul Revere's Ride." Encourage them to find and read the entire poem, either on the Internet or in a book. Then have them create a time line showing the most important events.

Fluency
Point out that ballads have a specific rhythm pattern, mainly because many of them were originally sung. Model the rhythm of "Paul Revere's Ride" by reading one stanza aloud. Then invite students to rehearse a stanza of their choosing to share with a partner.

Develop Oral Language
Have students work in small groups to practice reading the ballad aloud. Encourage them to pay attention to the rhythm pattern as they read. Then have students use the tune of a popular song to go with the words of the ballad. Encourage the groups to perform the ballad.

Writing

Ask partners to select a historical figure and list some of his or her accomplishments. Next, have students arrange the most interesting events in chronological order. Then challenge partners to write a ballad about the person.

Name _____   Date _____

[from] Paul Revere's Ride
by Henry Wadsworth Longfellow

Listen, my children, and you shall hear
Of the midnight ride of Paul Revere,
On the eighteenth of April, in Seventy-five;
Hardly a man is now alive
Who remembers that famous day and year.

He said to his friend, "If the British march
By land or sea from the town to-night,
Hang a lantern aloft in the belfry arch
Of the North Church tower as a signal light,—
One, if by land, and two, if by sea;
And I on the opposite shore will be,
Ready to ride and spread the alarm
Through every Middlesex village and farm,
For the country folk to be up and to arm."

Then he said, "Good-night!" and with
    muffled oar
Silently rowed to the Charlestown shore,
Just as the moon rose over the bay,
Where swinging wide at her moorings lay
The Somerset, British man-of-war;
A phantom ship, with each mast and spar
Across the moon like a prison bar,
And a huge black hulk, that was magnified
By its own reflection in the tide.

Meanwhile, his friend, through alley
    and street
Wanders and watches with eager ears,
Till in the silence around him he hears
The muster of men at the barrack door,
The sound of arms, and the tramp of feet,
And the measured tread of the grenadiers,
Marching down to their boats on the shore.

Then he climbed the tower of the
    Old North Church,
By the wooden stairs, with stealthy tread,
To the belfry-chamber overhead,
And startled the pigeons from their perch
On the sombre rafters, that round
    him made
Masses and moving shapes of shade,—
By the trembling ladder, steep and tall,
To the highest window in the wall,
Where he paused to listen and look down
A moment on the roofs of the town,
And the moonlight flowing over all.

Understand the Poem

[from] Paul Revere's Ride: Assessment

Think about the poem. Then answer the questions. Fill in the circle next to the correct answer.

1. What kinds of lights were to be used as signals?
Ⓐ candles
Ⓑ torches
Ⓒ bulbs
Ⓓ lanterns

2. What happened after Paul Revere rowed across the water?
Ⓐ A friend spied on the British.
Ⓑ He got on his horse and sounded the alarm.
Ⓒ He rowed out to a ship.
Ⓓ He climbed a ladder.

3. A "phantom ship" probably looks
Ⓐ large.
Ⓑ ghostly.
Ⓒ bright.
Ⓓ invisible.

4. Longfellow wrote the poem
Ⓐ to tell about a famous person in history.
Ⓑ to get people to ride horses.
Ⓒ to share information about a war.
Ⓓ to tell an amusing story.

5. How were the British going to attack?
Ⓐ by train
Ⓑ by horse
Ⓒ by land
Ⓓ by sea

6. What word best describes Paul Revere and his friend?
Ⓐ powerful
Ⓑ dishonorable
Ⓒ heroic
Ⓓ ferocious

7. Why is this poem a ballad?

_____

_____

_____

Name _____   Date _____

Words in Context

Use other words in the sentences to help you find the missing word.

✎ **Read each sentence. Find a word from the box to complete it. Then write the word on the line.**

| grenadiers magnified moorings muffled muster phantom sombre stealthy |

1. The _____ stood quietly with their rifles in hand.

2. They had just been called to _____ and gathered in rows.

3. The men walked in a _____ manner, not wanting to make any sounds.

4. One man began to cough, so he quickly _____ the sound with his hand so that no one would hear.

5. The glowing moon cast _____ shadows on the ground.

6. The captain looked through an eyeglass that _____ the scene below.

7. It looked like the enemy ships were sailing into the bay, so their

_____ would be close by.

8. The soldiers became quite _____ since they knew the battle would soon begin.

[from] **Mending Wall**

**Poetry Skill:
Free Verse Poetry**

Standard
Identify a free verse poem

Explore Free Verse Poetry
Invite students to read the poem and ask how it differs from other poems they have read. Help them note that this poem does not rhyme. Explain to the students that this poem is an example of free verse poetry. Explain that this style of poetry has no set length or rhyme scheme. Point out that free verse poetry does not have any rules—the poet decides how the poem should look, feel, and sound. Tell students that poets use imagery in their free verse poetry to help readers create a mental picture in their head.

Vocabulary

abreast–side by side
gaps–openings
mischief–troublemaking
notion–an idea
offense–hurting someone's feelings
savage–a fierce person
spell–words that have magic power

Summary

A neighbor thinks that "Good fences make good neighbors," but the poet thinks differently.

Read the Poem

Introduce the Poem
Ask students to brainstorm the purpose of walls and fences. Have students write their ideas on stone-shaped construction paper cutouts. As students share their ideas, tape the stones on a wall to form an image of a wall. Then invite students to listen to a poem about two men in New England who are mending a wall to see how each feels about the structure.

Introduce the Vocabulary
Divide the class into seven groups. Assign each group a vocabulary word. Have them find the word in the dictionary and write all the definitions on stone-shaped cutouts, like those in Introduce the Poem. Invite groups to share their findings as they add them to the classroom wall.

During Reading

Read the poem aloud to students.

After Reading

Questions
1. How does the poet feel about the wall? (*He does not think the wall is necessary.*)
2. To what does the poet compare the sizes of the rocks in the wall? (*bread loaves and balls*)
3. What is one reason the poet gives why the wall is not needed? (*They do not have cows to keep from wandering.*)

Fluency
Point out that free verse poetry can seem difficult to read because it seems to lack a rhythm or beat that is easy to hear. Explain that the tone of the reader's voice and the pace at which the poem is read are important as they help create the mental image for the listener. Suggest that partners discuss the tone and speed they think are appropriate and then rehearse several lines.

Writing

Remind students that "Mending Wall" is a free verse poem—the poet simply wrote his thoughts down to tell how he felt and what he saw. Invite students to write their own free verse poem that tells about a thought or feeling. Encourage them to just write the ideas that pop into their head.

[from] Mending Wall
by Robert Frost

Something there is that doesn't love a wall,
That sends the frozen-ground-swell under it,
And spills the upper boulders in the sun,
And makes gaps even two can pass abreast.
No one has seen them made
    or heard them made,
But at spring mending-time
    we find them there.
I let my neighbor know beyond the hill;
And on a day we meet to walk the line
And set the wall between us once again.
We keep the wall between us as we go.
To each the boulders that have fallen to each.
And some are loaves
    and some so nearly balls
We have to use a spell to make them balance:
"Stay where you are
    until our backs are turned!"
We wear our fingers rough
    with handling them.
Oh, just another kind of out-door game,
One on a side. It comes to little more:
There where it is we do not need the wall:
He is all pine and I am apple orchard.
My apple trees will never get across
And eat the cones under his pines, I tell him.
He only says,
    "Good fences make good neighbors."

Spring is the mischief in me, and I wonder
If I could put a notion in his head:
"Why do they make good neighbors? Isn't it
Where there are cows?
But here there are no cows.
Before I built a wall I'd ask to know
What I was walling in or walling out,
And to whom I was like to give offense.
Something there is that doesn't love a wall,
That wants it down." I see him there
Bringing a stone grasped firmly by the top
In each hand,
    like an old-stone savage armed.
He moves in darkness as it seems to me
Not of woods only and the shade of trees.
He will not go behind his father's saying,
And he likes having thought of it so well
He says again,
    "Good fences make good neighbors."

Understand the Poem

[from] Mending Wall: Assessment

Think about the poem. Then answer the questions. Fill in the circle next to the correct answer.

1. What kind of wall is in the poem?
- Ⓐ a rock wall
- Ⓑ a brick wall
- Ⓒ a dirt wall
- Ⓓ a tree wall

2. When do the men mend the wall?
- Ⓐ after summer
- Ⓑ before winter
- Ⓒ after spring
- Ⓓ after winter

3. A "notion" is
- Ⓐ a fright.
- Ⓑ a thread.
- Ⓒ an idea.
- Ⓓ a concern.

4. The poet's message in this poem is
- Ⓐ that walls need mending often.
- Ⓑ that neighbors should help each other.
- Ⓒ that old habits often outlast their usefulness.
- Ⓓ that neighbors should keep to themselves.

5. You can conclude that the poet's neighbor
- Ⓐ respects his father's opinions.
- Ⓑ is not interested in the poet's thoughts.
- Ⓒ does not want the poet on his property.
- Ⓓ is not interested in keeping the wall together.

6. What could you infer about the poet?
- Ⓐ He does not care for the hard work of lifting stones.
- Ⓑ He does not think a wall is necessary between good neighbors.
- Ⓒ He would like to have cows on his property.
- Ⓓ He does not care for his neighbor.

7. What does the poet mean when he says that his neighbor "moves in darkness"?

_____

_____

Name _____   Date _____

Homographs

Homographs are words that have the same spelling but different meanings. Use words in the sentence to help you choose the correct meaning of a word.

Example: ship
Meaning A: a large boat
Meaning B: to send or mail things

Read each sentence. What does the word in dark print mean? Write the letter for the meaning of the word.

gaps
Meaning A: openings
Meaning B: passes through the mountains

_____ **1.** The squirrels climbed into the garden through the **gaps** in the fence.

_____ **2.** Many roads were closed in the mountains during the winter because the **gaps** were covered with snow.

spell
Meaning A: words that have magic power
Meaning B: to say or write the letters in a word

_____ **3.** Some English words are hard to **spell**.

_____ **4.** "Abracadabra" is often used in a **spell**.

notion
Meaning A: an idea
Meaning B: thread or trim used in sewing

_____ **5.** Mr. West had a **notion** to read a book.

_____ **6.** Soon Li bought fabric, thread, buttons, and another **notion** to make a dress.

offense
Meaning A: hurting someone's feelings
Meaning B: attempting to score

_____ **7.** Rita did not mean to give **offense** when she did not eat the food.

_____ **8.** The team that has the ball will play **offense**.

Eldorado

Poetry Skill: Rhythm

Standard
Identify rhythm

Explore Meter
Explain to students that many poems have a specific rhythm, or beat. The beat is called *meter*. Then read the first six lines of the poem, stressing the syllables to emphasize the beat. Discuss the pattern students hear. Next, have partners review the poem and record the number of syllables in each line to confirm the pattern of the poem.

Vocabulary

bedight–dressed
gallant–heroic
journeyed–traveled
pilgrim–a wanderer
seek–search

Research Base

"**S**tudents who are immersed in the vibrant sounds of poetry will write better poetry themselves; what's more, they are more likely to develop a lifetime appreciation for poetry."
(*Guiding Readers and Writers: Grades 3–6*, p. 419)

Summary

Edgar Allan Poe blends music and poetry in this tale of a knight who searches for wealth, only to find that it cannot be found in this world.

Read the Poem

Introduce the Poem

Tell students that Eldorado was the imaginary place that early Spanish and English explorers looked for because it was fabled to be a city of great wealth. Explain that Poe wrote the words, which were originally made into a song, about the California gold rush. Ask them to listen to the poem to find images of what Eldorado means to Poe.

Introduce the Vocabulary

Write the vocabulary words and the definitions on the board. Lead students in a brief discussion of the words. Then have students create a crossword puzzle with the words using the graph on page 11. Challenge students to write sentences as clues to complete the puzzle.

During Reading

Read the poem aloud to students.

After Reading

Questions

1. How does the poet use images of light and dark in the poem? (*Things that have to do with light represent happiness and life. Things that are dark and shady represent evil and death.*)
2. What had the knight been searching for his whole life? (*a land of great wealth*)
3. Does Poe think that the men who went to the gold rush would find Eldorado? Explain. (*No, because this one dies before finding it or even coming close to gold.*)

Fluency

Point out the em-dashes to students. Explain that they signal that a reader should pause. Model how to fluently read several lines that have an em-dash. Then invite partners to rehearse the same lines.

Develop Oral Language

Have partners read the poem chorally.

Writing

Ask students to write a paragraph or a poem that describes their vision of Eldorado. Have them draw a picture to match.

Eldorado
by Edgar Allan Poe

Gaily bedight,
A gallant knight,
In sunshine and in shadow,
Had journeyed long,
Singing a song,
In search of Eldorado.
But he grew old—
This knight so bold—
And o'er his heart a shadow
Fell as he found
No spot of ground
That looked like Eldorado.

And, as his strength
Failed him at length,
He met a pilgrim shadow—
"Shadow," said he,
"Where can it be—
This land of Eldorado?"
"Over the Mountains
Of the Moon,
Down the Valley of the Shadow,
Ride, boldly ride,"
The shade replied,—
"If you seek for Eldorado."

Understand the Poem

Eldorado: Assessment

✎ **Think about the poem. Then answer the questions. Fill in the circle next to the correct answer.**

1. What is the knight looking for?
Ⓐ the shadow
Ⓑ a friend
Ⓒ a place
Ⓓ his horse

2. What happened to the knight after he rode for some time?
Ⓐ He sold his armor.
Ⓑ He grew tired.
Ⓒ He was attacked.
Ⓓ He found Eldorado.

3. The knight meets a "pilgrim shadow." A "pilgrim" is probably
Ⓐ a settler.
Ⓑ frightening.
Ⓒ a traveler.
Ⓓ familiar.

4. The poem is mostly about
Ⓐ a lifelong search.
Ⓑ a handsome knight.
Ⓒ a shadow.
Ⓓ a beautiful place.

5. You can conclude that
Ⓐ the knight is too young to reach Eldorado.
Ⓑ knights are not allowed in Eldorado.
Ⓒ the shadow is lying to the knight.
Ⓓ the shadow has seen Eldorado.

6. Which of these is most likely true at the end of the poem?
Ⓐ The knight travels with the shadow.
Ⓑ The knight returns to his home.
Ⓒ The knight is near the end of his life.
Ⓓ The knight and the shadow become friends.

7. What does the shadow in the poem represent?

_____

_____

Lesson 19 • Eldorado: Poem Assessment
Poetry: Grade 6, SV 9896-5

Synonyms

A synonym is a word that means the same or almost the same as another word.
Examples: start—begin   happy—glad

Read each sentence. Find a word in the box that means the same
or almost the same as the word in dark print. Write the word on the line.

amazement	bedight	exhausted	gallant	fame
journeyed	pilgrim	remainder	seek	shade

1. The knight had **traveled** a long way. _____

2. He was **tired**. _____

3. Now poorly **dressed**, his clothes clearly once had
been trimmed in gold and fur. _____

4. He paused in the **shadow** of a tree to rest. _____

5. A **wanderer**, who was walking along the same road,
also stopped to rest. _____

6. The man said, "Greetings, **brave** knight." _____

7. "For what do you **search**?" the man asked. _____

8. "I am looking for gold and **glory**," said the knight. _____

9. To the knight's **surprise**, the wanderer just laughed. _____

10. "You will continue to search for the **rest** of your life,"
chuckled the man as he continued on his way. _____

Looking for Trouble

Poetry Skill: Dialect

Standard
Identify the use of figurative language (simile, metaphor, personification, dialect)

Explore Dialect
Explain to students that dialect is a form of figurative language used to develop characters and enhance tone. Discuss that people who live in the same area or share the same culture also share language habits. After sharing examples of dialect familiar to students, point out that poets try to show this by writing the way they hear people speak. Explain that the words may be misspelled or have missing letters. The poet may use words and expressions unique to the particular culture. Have students look at the poem and highlight the words and phrases that are examples of dialect.

Vocabulary

annoy–to bother
coy–acting quietly to deceive
influence–a person who has the power to produce an effect
lectured–spoke to
rascal–a bad, dishonest person
twiddled–moved in a circle

Summary

A boy has a friend who always gets into trouble because the friend is always looking for fun things to do.

Read the Poem

Introduce the Poem
Lead students in a discussion of what a good friend is and how one would act. Allow time for them to share stories about times that friends have been especially thoughtful. Then invite students to listen to a poet describe a friend to see if this friend is thoughtful.

Introduce the Vocabulary
Write the vocabulary words and the definitions on separate cards. Pin them to a bulletin board in any order. Then say a sentence with a vocabulary word and ask a volunteer to find the word and the definition that matches.

During Reading

Read the poem aloud to students.

After Reading

Questions
1. Who is telling the story? (*the poet*)
2. Why did the father not like the poet's friend? (*The friend always got into trouble.*)
3. Why do you think the poet did not listen to his father? (*Accept reasonable answers.*)

Fluency
Point out to students that the quotation marks signal that a person is talking. Discuss how the characters are feeling in the different parts of the poem and how they might say those words. Challenge partners to rehearse the different parts as if they were the characters in the poem.

Develop Oral Language
Assign students to groups of three and invite them to read the poem in parts.

Writing

Invite students to write a paragraph or a poem describing something memorable they have done with a good friend. Encourage them to use words and phrases in the dialect that they speak among their peers.

Name _____   Date _____

Looking for Trouble
by Anonymous

"Who is it you'll be with today
When you go down to the park to play?
What's his name?" I heard Father say.

"Yeah, whatshisname. You know. That guy."
When I talk to Dad I never lie.
I wouldn't even want to try.

"Did you say Billy Beanalee?"
Now Dad was looking straight at me,
And I nodded yes. "Oh, no! not he!"

"Not that rascal!" Father said.
"You'll come home injured, or, worse yet, dead!"
He was holding and shaking his head.

"He's not a good influence, that boy!
There's not a soul he can't annoy,"
Dad said. "He's too clever, and he's coy!"

So I left my father in a worried way
And went off to join my friend in play.
I was late, and Billy had come halfway.

"I bet they lectured you back there,"
He said. "But gosh, it isn't fair
That I get more trouble than my share."

"Let's just sit," he said. "Not do a thing
And hope that my luck doesn't bring
Us trouble . . . or boredom . . . or anything."

He twiddled his thumbs, gave a yawn or two,
Then said, "I'll tell you what we'll do.
I'll find trouble and run it off for you!"

Name _____   Date _____

Looking for Trouble: Assessment

Think about the poem. Then answer the questions. Fill in the circle next to the correct answer.

1. Who does not like Billy Beanalee?
   - Ⓐ the poet
   - Ⓑ the poet's mother
   - Ⓒ the poet's friend
   - Ⓓ the poet's father

2. What happened when the poet was late?
   - Ⓐ He ran home.
   - Ⓑ He called his friend.
   - Ⓒ His friend met him halfway.
   - Ⓓ His friend got in trouble.

3. A person who "annoys" would
   - Ⓐ be a pest.
   - Ⓑ be helpful.
   - Ⓒ be cheerful.
   - Ⓓ be angry.

4. The poet wrote the poem
   - Ⓐ to tell how friends should act.
   - Ⓑ to describe a game to play.
   - Ⓒ to share a humorous story.
   - Ⓓ to encourage children to act appropriately.

5. Why did the friend twiddle his thumbs at the end of the poem?
   - Ⓐ He thought of a way to get into trouble.
   - Ⓑ The poet's father had come.
   - Ⓒ He was bored.
   - Ⓓ The poet had to leave.

6. Which word would NOT be used to describe the friend?
   - Ⓐ prankster
   - Ⓑ well-liked
   - Ⓒ energetic
   - Ⓓ troublesome

7. Is the poet's friend a good friend? Explain.

_____

_____

Name _____   Date _____

Dictionary Skills

A dictionary tells how to say a word and what it means.

___

Look at the pronunciation key. Then circle the word that matches the pronunciation.

a	add	i	it	o͝o	took	oi	oil
ā	ace	ī	ice	o͞o	pool	ou	pout
â	care	o	odd	u	up	ng	ring
ä	palm	ō	open	û	burn	th	thin
e	end	ô	order	yo͞o	fuse	t͟h	this
ē	equal					zh	vision

ə = { a in *above*   e in *sicken*   i in *possible*   o in *melon*   u in *circus* }

1. (nod´ id)   noted   nodded   knotted

2. (sōl)   school   sold   soul

3. (ras´ kəl)   rascal   wrestle   resale

4. (in´ jûrd)   injury   injured   edged

5. (in´ flo͞o əns)   inflows   influxes   influence

6. (lek´ chərd)   leaked   liter   lectured

7. (bôrd´ əm)   boredom   boarding   burden

8. (twid´ əld)   tweeted   twiddled   twinkled

Choose four of the circled words above. Write sentences with them.

9. _____

_____

_____

_____

___

Poetry Grade 6 • Answer Key

Page 8
1. C
2. A
3. D
4. C
5. A
6. B
7. Longfellow is comparing his sad mood to a dreary day. He wants to cry tears like the clouds cry rain.

Page 16
1. C
2. B
3. D
4. B
5. A
6. D
7. The mood is light and humorous. The poet uses made-up words like "kerwhacky" and "Paky" for humor, He also plays with words at the end by saying that the dinosaur is a bonehead.

Page 17
1. B
2. A
3. B
4. A
5. A
6. B
7. B
8. A

Page 20
1. C
2. D
3. B
4. A
5. B
6. C
7. The Raggedy Man does not like bees and is saying that no matter how long a bee is around, it is too long.

Page 21
1. fagged—tired
2. slouchy—physically showing being tired by walking or sitting bent over
3. wuz—the word "was"
4. buzzin'—buzzing
5. 'Ithout —the word "without"
6. o'—the word "of"
7. an' nen—the words "and then"
8. muntained—maintained

Page 24
1. D
2. B
3. C
4. D
5. A
6. B
7. The animal characters talk, and a person who has a huge hat lives in a tree.

Page 25
1. luminous
2. grant
3. creatures
4. airy
5. charmingly
6. silently
7. large
8. corkscrew
9. amazement
10. plainer

Page 28
1. D
2. B
3. D
4. C
5. A
6. D
7. Most likely answer: Don't judge people by the way they look. Judge them by what they do and say.

Page 29
Definitions may vary.
1. cheerful; happy
2. incessantly; nonstop
3. endless; without end
4. patiently; doing without complaint
5. knowledgeable; full of knowledge
6. hopeful; full of hope
7. clueless; not having a hint about a problem

Page 32
1. C
2. A
3. B
4. D
5. B
6. C
7. Answers will vary. Accept reasonable answers and explanations.

Page 33
1. When I am bored, I write poems.
2. Keesha read a new book of tall tales.
3. No one is allowed to talk during a fire drill.
4. Where is your new sleigh?
5. I cannot wait for the flowers to grow.
6. We are studying cells in our science class.
7. Do you know how to go to the library?
8. The air is nice and fresh today.

Page 36
1. D
2. B
3. D
4. A
5. B
6. D
7. Answers will vary. The poet says that the fearful trip is over and a prize has been won, causing the people to celebrate, but at the same time, the Captain is cold and dead, causing grief and tears.

Page 37
1. F
2. H
3. A
4. G
5. I
6. B
7. D
8. J
9. C
10. E
11.–14. Sentences will vary.

Page 40
1. B
2. A
3. C
4. C
5. A
6. B
7. The mood of the poem is light-hearted or melancholy.

Poetry Grade 6 • Answer Key

Page 41
Answers will vary. Possible answers are given.
1. green as in a grassy area
2. sport as in play
3. play as to have fun
4. folk as in people
5. rest as in sleep
6. ones as in dollar bills
7. ring as in a sound
8. hand as to help out

Page 44
1. A
2. A
3. A
4. D
5. B
6. B
7. He misses his childhood days.

Page 45
Across
3. appassionato
6. cast
7. insidious
8. parlour
Down
1. clamour
2. betrays
4. poised
5. vista

Page 48
1. A
2. B
3. C
4. D
5. B
6. A
7. to compare two opposite nouns or things

Page 49
1. J
2. H
3. E
4. C
5. B
6. F
7. I
8. A
9. D
10. G
11.–14. Sentences will vary.

Page 52
1. C
2. A
3. C
4. B
5. A
6. D
7. Most likely answer: Even though the children had grown and left, making the poet sad, he understood that life continued and was happy to have a child with him.

Page 53
1. playmates
2. inquired
3. accepted
4. gravelled
5. lindens
6. familiar
7. pressed

Page 56
1. C
2. A
3. B
4. B
5. A
6. C
7. Answers will vary, but should reflect problems faced by electric appliances not working and by not being able to use transportation due to icy road conditions.

Page 57
1. wand
2. hosts
3. cruel
4. descended
5. endeavors
6. graceful
7. denied
8. complete
9. complete, cruel, denied, descended, endeavors, graceful, hosts, wand

Page 60
1. B
2. C
3. A
4. B
5. D
6. C
7. The cat appears not to have a home and seems to be hungry. In such situations, animals would probably not have much hope.

Page 61
1. E
2. H
3. J
4. A
5. I
6. B
7. G
8. C
9. F
10. D
11. Sentences will vary.

Page 64
1. C
2. A
3. B
4. D
5. A
6. B
7. The gardener liked the weeds but pulled them up anyway because they were not planned to be part of the garden.

Page 65
1. depending
2. voted
3. ignored
4. friend
5. talkative
6. gardeners
7. cowered
8. actively
9. cultured
10. prim
11.–13. Sentences will vary.

Page 68
1. C
2. B
3. A
4. A
5. D
6. B
7. Answers will vary.

Poetry Grade 6 • Answer Key

Page 69
1. B
2. A
3. B
4. A
5. A
6. B
7. B
8. A

Page 72
1. B
2. A
3. D
4. B
5. A
6. D
7. Answers will vary.

Page 73
1. soil toil
2. sages' wages
3. pedaling meddling
4. a mellow fellow
5. leaves thieves
6. a shore lore store

Page 76
1. C
2. B
3. D
4. A
5. C
6. B
7. The first point of view is the all-knowing (omniscient) narrator. The second point of view is the rat that is compared to Julius Caesar. The poem shares his commentary, which is noted in quotation marks.

Page 77
1. D
2. I
3. A
4. J
5. G
6. E
7. B
8. F
9. C
10. H
11. Sentences will vary.

Page 80
1. D
2. A
3. B
4. A
5. D
6. C
7. It tells a story about a famous person as well as a famous event. It is written in stanzas that have a specific rhythm.

Page 81
1. grenadiers
2. muster
3. stealthy
4. muffled
5. phantom
6. magnified
7. moorings
8. sombre

Page 84
1. A
2. D
3. C
4. C
5. A
6. B
7. Most likely answer: The neighbor was stuck in the past and did not want to consider a new concept—there was no need for a wall.

Page 85
1. A
2. B
3. B
4. A
5. A
6. B
7. A
8. B

Page 88
1. C
2. B
3. C
4. A
5. D
6. C
7. The shadow represents death.

Page 89
1. journeyed
2. exhausted
3. bedight
4. shade
5. pilgrim
6. gallant
7. seek
8. fame
9. amazement
10. remainder

Page 92
1. D
2. C
3. A
4. C
5. C
6. B
7. Answers will vary.

Page 93
1. nodded
2. soul
3. rascal
4. injured
5. influence
6. lectured
7. boredom
8. twiddled
9. Sentences will vary.

Reference
Fountas, Irene C. and Pinnell, Gay Su. 2001. *Guiding Readers and Writers: Grades 3–6.* Portsmouth, NH: Heinemann.